HEBEWS

Dana Congdon

ISBN: 978-1-942521-52-5

Available from:

Christian Testimony Ministry
4424 Huguenot Road
Richmond, Virginia 23235

www.christiantestimonyministry.com

Printed in USA

CONTENTS

A STRONG EXHORTATION

Hebrews 1:1-4—God, after He spoke long ago to the fathers in the prophets in many portions and in many ways, in these last days has spoken to us in His Son, whom He appointed heir of all things, through whom also He made the world. And He is the radiance of His glory and the exact representation of His nature, and upholds all things by the word of His power. When He had made purification of sins, He sat down at the right hand of the Majesty on high, having become as much better than the angels, as He has inherited a more excellent name than they.

Hebrews 6:17-20—In the same way God, desiring even more to show to the heirs of the promise the unchangeableness of His purpose, interposed with an oath, so that by two unchangeable things in which it is impossible for God to lie, we who have taken refuge would have strong encouragement to take hold of the hope set before us. This hope we have as an anchor of the soul, a hope both sure and steadfast and one which enters within the veil, where Jesus has entered as a forerunner for us, having become a high priest forever according to the order of Melchizedek.

Hebrews 10:32-11:2—But remember the former days, when, after being enlightened, you endured a great conflict of sufferings, partly by being made a public spectacle through reproaches and tribulations, and partly by becoming sharers with those who were so treated. For you showed sympathy to the prisoners and accepted joyfully the seizure of your property, knowing that you have for yourselves a better possession and a lasting one. Therefore, do not throw away your confidence, which has a great reward. For you have need of endurance, so that when you have done the will of God, you may receive what was promised.

For yet in a very little while, He who is coming will come, and will not delay. But my righteous one shall live by faith; and if he shrinks back, my soul has no pleasure in him.

But we are not of those who shrink back to destruction, but of those who have faith to the preserving of the soul. Now faith is the assurance of things hoped for, the conviction of things not seen. For by it the men of old gained [the testimony].

*Hebrews 12:25-29—See to it that you do not refuse Him who is speaking. For if those did not escape when they refused him who warned them on earth, much less will we escape who turn away from Him who warns from heaven. And His voice shook the earth then, but now He has promised, saying, "*YET ONCE MORE I WILL SHAKE NOT ONLY THE EARTH, BUT ALSO THE HEAVEN.*" This expression, "Yet once more, denotes the removing of those things which can be shaken, as of created things, so that those things which cannot be shaken may remain. Therefore, since we receive a kingdom which cannot be shaken, let us [have grace] by which we may offer to God an acceptable service with reverence and awe; for our God is a consuming fire.*

Hebrews 13:22—But I urge you, brethren, bear with this word of exhortation, for I have written to you briefly.

Let's pray:

Our Father, we thank You so much for the precious word of God that we have before us, and as we gather together for these days we thank You for the rest and fellowship, for the remembrance of Your faithfulness over the years. And we pray that all these benefits and blessings, as we are gathered together, may fortify us for the race that lies ahead. We pray that You will help us to understand and especially to obey that which we hear from Your throne. We pray that these days will be an encounter under an open heaven when we may see our Lord Jesus clearly before us and run the race with Him before us. We ask for Your help, for refreshing of tired bodies, and for opening of hearts, stubborn hearts, for a clear seeing in our spirit as we fellowship together in this time. Thank You, Lord, that we can depend on You for all that we need. You have been made to us wisdom, righteousness, and sanctification, and redemption. We take our full portion in Christ and we pray in His precious name. Amen.

One of the great lessons that we learn from the book of Hebrews over all is that God sends a strong word of encouragement before He brings on a strong shaking. We see this from the context of this letter to the Hebrews. When this letter was written, the ground was already trembling, not only among the Diaspora, that is the dispersed Jews throughout Asia, Macedonia and Greece, and so forth, but most especially in Palestine, in Jerusalem, and in Galilee. The ground was already shaking when this strong encouragement was given.

When you read the account of Josephus and other historians, you realize most Bible scholars believe this time was just before 70 AD, and there was great chaos not only in Jerusalem but in Judea as a whole. During the days since Jesus had lived upon this earth, Judaism was falling into greater and greater splits and fights and sects. They were forming groups. False messiahs were being raised up, and all kind of zealous counter attacks were attempted upon Rome. They were building Masada, and they were hiding out in the wilderness among the Essenes. There was a lot of confusion, a lot of chaos, a lot of division, and the Jews were killing each other by the thousands every year just over different sectarian differences that they had among them. The day was growing ripe for that time in 70 AD when Titus came and destroyed what was left of all of the system of Judaism, and a million and a half Jews were killed. He came and destroyed the city of Jerusalem, its temple, its altars, its system, its priesthood, its sacrifices. The whole thing went down in 70 AD, and the tremors on the ground could be felt before it happened.

We do not know what happened to all those Jews but more than that, what happened to the Jewish Christians? We know when Paul returned on his last journey back to Jerusalem with a gift for the saints in Judea, it was about 55 AD. And it was clearly stated that they were still zealous for the Law, and that means an awful lot. It does not just mean they were keeping the Ten Commandments; it means they were continuing in the traditions, in the sacrifices, in the centrality of the temple, and all of these kind of things along with their belief in Jesus the Messiah.

Paul had been martyred by the time of the writing of this letter. Now some people believe this was a letter written by Paul, and it is possible. The language is quite different, but it is possible that through another writer he dictated it and so it came out differently. Some believe that originally it was in Hebrew and later translated into Greek but that does not seem to be the case. If it was Paul it was certainly a different sort of spirit, but one could imagine as he is ripening there in jail and waiting for his martyrdom that perhaps something like this was written.

But Paul's message was not to the Jewish Christians. He was sent to the Gentiles, and as we all know Paul's universal gospel which was so well received in the world in the Roman Empire of those days was really not that well received among the Jewish Christians. They put up with Paul, and of course even when Paul came to Jerusalem on that last visit before he was thrown into jail, he told them everything that the Lord had been doing in those places and it says, "And they all praised God for what He was doing." So they were in full accord with the evangelism of the Gentile world, but they were having a problem with what to do with being a Christian and a Jew. They had heard stories that Paul was going around telling the Jewish parents not to circumcise their children or to observe any of the traditions of the Jews. They were very upset about this and wanted to know what was happening.

In any case I believe that Paul had already been martyred by this time. Now what is going to happen to these Hebrew Christians, not only in the Diaspora where they spoke Greek but in Jerusalem? They had been together almost forty years, a generation, and they had two large contingents, as James said in Acts 21. There were tens of thousands of Jewish Christians in Jerusalem, and a large number of them were Greek speaking and a large number Hebrew speaking. Thank God they were holding together as the church. It was a wonderful testimony, but they were going through some troubling times. And what is going to happen as the ground begins to shake? What are the Christians going to do in that atmosphere? Or more specifically, who will be raised up to speak to them during those very difficult times? Somebody needs to give them strong encouragement.

A STRONG EXHORTATION

The word *exhortation* is an old English word, and it is the same in the Greek. It means two things—"encouragement and warning" both at the same time. It is a double-barreled word. An exhortation is something that is a positive encouragement and a negative warning, both at the same time. And this whole letter to the Hebrews is a strong encouragement, a strong exhortation. It is interesting the way our translators usually lop down on the side of the positive. So the New American Standard Translation usually says encouragement, "that you may have strong encouragement." But take the full dosage; it is a strong warning and a strong encouragement. Can you handle it both at the same time?

Who can usher this strong exhortation at such a time as this when the ground is beginning to shake, when the Roman army is gathering and beginning to come down toward Jerusalem? Who can do this? For the Jews it cannot be some Gentile. It has got to be a Jew; it has got to be somebody familiar with the Law. Of course, it has got to be somebody who has come right through in grace. Who is such a person? Well I have my own idea, although it is not my own; many people believe it. But I believe this job of writing this letter fell to Joseph the Levite. Joseph the Levite, I believe, was just the man to write this book. Now if you do not believe that it is perfectly okay. You can be wrong. If you are right, then I am wrong. But it was certainly somebody like Joseph the Levite, if it was not him. Now perhaps you do not know him under the name Joseph the Levite because his name was also Barnabas.

In Acts 4:36 we have the first account of this man: "Now Joseph, a Levite of Cyprian birth (which means he came from Cyprus, so he was a Greek-speaking Jew), who was also called Barnabas by the apostles (which translated means Son of Exhortation) and who owned a tract of land, sold it and brought the money and laid it at the apostles' feet."

Then in chapter 11:23 Barnabas is in Antioch encouraging the church: "Then when Barnabas arrived and witnessed the grace of God, he rejoiced and began to exhort them all with resolute heart to remain true to the Lord; for he was a good man, and full of the Holy Spirit and of faith. And considerable numbers were brought to the Lord."

You probably know that Barnabas' life was one of encouragement and that he introduced Paul to the church in Jerusalem. Now here we see this wonderful brother going to Antioch and he sees what is going on. His heart senses that this is from the Lord, and he immediately begins to bring strong exhortation to those newly born saints. And many more were saved during his brief stay there. He was a man of strong exhortation, "the Son of Exhortation" as he was called. And I believe he was the man who was just right for this situation.

Where was Barnabas' home? We know it was in Cyprus originally because he sold his property. We do not know exactly what that means, but for sure he had never left Jerusalem and was always received in Jerusalem by the saints there. He was originally sent out from Jerusalem, and yet he was at home in Antioch.

Later he worked with Saul of Taurus for more than a year in Antioch. He was welcomed in Antioch among the Jews and the Gentiles. And of course, because of his journeys with Paul he was also welcomed among the churches in the Diaspora, Cyprus, and Asia Minor; at least that far. So this Barnabas was a man raised up for such a time.

In the midst of the shaking there arose one who brought strong encouragement. Now if it was not Barnabas, then just leave it like this. God had to raise up somebody just before 70 AD who could bring that kind of strong exhortation to the saints and release them from the bondage they were in. This strong word of exhortation had to shake them loose, to shake loose from them that which would soon be shaken. This exhortation was so strong in the book of Hebrews that those who read it and heeded it were shaken out of the shadows of those traditions and vestiges they were holding on to. And we find a wonderful and helpful phrase to us: "He shook them out of the shadows and into the living." He brought them into a living faith, even as he talks about in chapter 11. It is a living faith that pleases God. It is out of the shadows into a living faith that brought them back before the living God.

In chapter 3, when the writer to the Hebrews says "the living God," he is making a point by adding "living" there because all the Jews believed in God, but were they related to a living God? So chapter 3:12 is one of several examples in Hebrews: "Take care, brethren, that there not be in any one of you an evil, unbelieving heart that falls away from the living God."

This exhortation is meant to shake loose those things that cause us to fall away from a living relationship with a living God by living faith. And of course, through this we enter in by His living word. "The word of God is living and active" (Hebrews 4:12). Oh, isn't it wonderful to have a living word; not just some letter that we are trying to observe in the shadows of effort? But a living word cuts and separates and sanctifies and sets us free. And He has even made them partakers who could walk in the new and living way that we find in Hebrews 10. Oh, how precious is the exhortation of the word of God!

LET US

I would like to talk briefly by way of introduction on this matter of the importance of the exhortative power of the word of God to bring us into some kind of maturity and snap us out of those things that hold onto us. And Barnabas or whoever it was who wrote this certainly gave us this meat of the word; it is that which matures people with strong warnings. But, of course, you know there are strong rewards, a strong stand in objectivity, and a strong experience in the Lord Himself. All of this is through the strength and message of maturity. One of the ways you can tell that something is an exhortation, especially unto maturity, is when it uses this exhortative phrase: "Let us." And of course you know that the book of Hebrews is full of "let us." All kind of passages have to do with "let us do this, let us do that."

We will just look at a few here. I have picked seven out of the fourteen that are found in the book of Hebrews.

"Therefore, let us fear, that after receiving these promises we do not unite them by faith and enter the rest." Then it goes on to say, "Let us enter the rest" (14:1).

"Therefore let us draw near to the throne of grace; let us be bold" (4:16).

"Therefore let us press on to maturity" (6:1). All the time this "let us" just means it is an exhortation, not just a request, not just a statement, but it is an exhortation.

"Let us draw near with a sincere heart in full assurance of faith" (10:22a).

"Let us run with patience the race that is set before us" (12:1b).

"Let us have grace that we may offer to God an acceptable service" (12:28b). You may have "gratitude"; grace can mean gratitude. In the midst of the shaking take His grace. Let's have grace; let's be full of grace and thanksgiving.

"Through Him then, let us continually offer up a sacrifice of praise to God" (13:15a).

I remember the first time I heard somebody teach the book of Hebrews. It was quite unusual because it was a Pentecostal preacher in a conference, and his subject was the importance of holiness. He used the book of Hebrews, and of course, you can imagine why because it is full of matters on holiness. But the thing that impressed me so much about that particular Pentecostal preacher was how much he showed the beauty of holiness. As a Christian we need to get used to this unfamiliar territory of holiness because it is altogether beautiful. And he pictured the beautiful, holy Christ, and then he pictured a beautiful, holy living way that has been opened before us. In every way he showed the beauty of holiness. The times I had heard holiness mentioned was like something that gave me the creeps a little bit. It was kind of tough, sort of austere. I had heard of an austere holiness, but a beautiful holiness! This man was enraptured in the holiness of Jesus. Isn't that wonderful! Surely this book of Hebrews is full of the beauty of holiness. Even the exhorter, whoever he may be, begins this strong word of exhortation by bringing the saints in through worship. He starts right off talking about the Lord Jesus and who He is and then brings in Psalm 8, that wonderful worship hymn. It is a worshipful experience.

FOUR ABSOLUTES

But I want to introduce the book by stating four absolutes that bring us to maturity. This book has absolutes in it. I am sorry for those of you who may be relativists and you do not believe in right and wrong, light and dark, and that sort of thing. It is very popular today not to believe in all that sort of thing. But to go on to maturity you have got to stand your ground on absolutes. One of the wonderful things about the Bible is that the word of God has absolutes. If you can believe it and cross over on these absolutes, they bring you to maturity. The word of God is strong. It necessitates us, in a sense, to stand by faith in the absolute truth of the word of God. And when we do that, then the Lord brings us into the reality of the experience. But the key at the starting place in looking at Hebrews sort of from the outside in is this. Are you ready to accept the absolutes that would bring us to maturity?

Jesus Is God

The first one is this: Jesus is God. That is where the writer starts. Now you may say, "That is no problem for me." Well, maybe this is more than a doctrine. Probably you know this because all of you have been through the book of Hebrews a number of times; you know all these things. Probably you know that in the background of this book that during the shaking time just before 70 AD there was a problem already evident among these Jewish Christians, and it grew until in the second century it was decided it was a heresy. What was that problem? From historical records that they have exhumed they found that a number of these Jewish Christians were Galilean Christians. These were Jews from Galilee who had been saved and believed that Jesus was the Messiah. They believed that Jesus was the suffering Servant predicted in Isaiah 53. They believed that their sins were forgiven through Jesus' death on the cross. They believed that Jesus was raised again from the dead, but they did not believe that Jesus was divine. They believed that He was a man. Now you say, "How can they work out the theology of salvation?" People do not always work that out. They accepted Jesus as their Savior and their Messiah. They were living in Messianic communities but they could not quite step over. I hope you can appreciate this. If you were a Jew and you had heard all your life that Jehovah, Jehovah is One. Then you suddenly hear somebody like Paul who comes along and says, "Jesus is divine; He the Son of God who existed before all creation." You say, "Wait a minute. Are you saying there are two Gods?" The mind cannot get around this whole problem. So among the Jewish community there were those who were Jewish Christians, truly Christians, and they really believed in Jesus, but they did not understand that Jesus was divine.

What does our dear brother do to bring them into maturity? He just cuts them right off at the knees. The opening statement of the book of Hebrews is "Jesus is God." He is the Son of God, the image of God, the expression of God, the nature of God. In Hebrews 1:3 it says, "He is the radiance of His glory and the exact representation of His nature, and upholds all things by the word of His power. When He had made purification of sins, He sat down at the right hand of the Majesty on high."

The writer cuts right through and says, "Jesus is the Son of God." Now if these Jews could cross that border, I hope you understand what would happen. What happens when everything gets shaken and the big shaking comes, and you do not understand that Jesus is God? That He is the Lord who is in control? That He is the Lamb who holds the scroll? That the shaking is by His permission and allowance? What happens when difficult times come but you do not have a high enough view of Jesus and you do not really see that He is God? You could fall apart. That is why it is so important to cross over on this.

If you do not think this is a problem today, then you do not understand the Christian problem today. I am going to make a broad-side statement which I cannot prove, but I am going to say that a large, large numbers of professors and various different Bible colleges and seminaries today no longer believe in the virgin birth of Jesus, no longer believe in His sinless life, no longer believe in the vicarious atonement of Jesus on the cross, nor do they believe that Jesus rose from the dead, and they are teaching all their students these things.

When I first went to seminary, different professors would preach in the area of Louisville, KY, and there was one guy that was so powerful, preaching the resurrection, preaching the gospel, and people got saved. This man had the gift. He had the words and everything. Then I took a class on John under him and I found out that he did not believe in the resurrection. I went up to him and asked him, "How can you preach the resurrection out there?" Basically what happens is that they change all the definitions so that they can say, "I believe in the resurrection. I believe in the virgin birth, I believe in this and that." But they just change it all. He does believe in the resurrection, a spiritual resurrection. But when he gets up before the people and preaches, he does not say that. When you hear that kind of stuff, it is so heady. It is such a problem among Christians today.

And one reason Christians cannot go on to maturity is because we have to come to grips with the all-sufficiency of Jesus Christ in His work and in the all-supremacy of Jesus Christ in what is happening around us or else we will fall apart. When the shaking comes, some people go back to their rosary. Some people say, "I worship Jesus but I had better check up with Mary again; she may hear my prayers." When things fall apart, some people believe in Jesus but they go back for a prophetic word from somebody. But here is the mark of somebody who is stepping toward maturity. They have made the crossover, and they believe Jesus is all-sufficient and He is all they need for their full salvation. They do not need to scramble, search, crawl, climb up a mountain, or believe in something extraneous. Jesus is God.

How do we know Jesus is God? It is something we see by revelation, isn't it? It does not make sense to man's mind. You can try to figure it out and play around with it, but it does not sound reasonable that there is God-God and Jesus-God. They are both God, yet they are both different. That only comes by revelation; you just see it and you know. But this crossover is so important in the survival of our lives.

In the book of Hebrews it has a particular impact. Here is the paradox. We have to establish that Jesus is the Son of God, all-sufficient, and then He can minister to us as the very human Jesus, the High Priest and Apostle. We have to understand that He is God before He can help us in His humanity. And the book of Hebrews is very much to do with Jesus helping us in His humanity. Of course, He is both Man and God. You will see that as we continue on.

This is the number one absolute. Jesus is God. If you can handle it, you cross over. If the Jews could handle that, when the shaking came, they could make it. They could hold on to Jesus as their all-sufficient Lord and make it through.

Once For All

The second absolute is this. If you come to maturity, you have got to believe that the work of Jesus was once for all. It was a one time perfect redemption; nothing more needed to be done. This goes along with the first one to a certain degree. But some of you may not have seen this in Hebrews in this way. Let's look at some verses that use this phrase "once for all."

"For it was fitting for us to have such a high priest, holy, innocent, undefiled, separated from sinners and exalted above the heavens; who does not need daily, like those high priests, to offer up sacrifices, first for His own sins and then for the sins of the people, because this He did once for all when He offered up Himself" (Hebrews 7:26-27).

This is the first use of this in this particular redemptive context. He does not have to do it again; it is once for all. It is a perfect finished work.

"And not through the blood of goats and calves, but through His own blood. He entered the holy place once for all, having obtained eternal redemption" (9:12).

"Otherwise, He would have needed to suffer often since the foundation of the world, but now once at the consummation of the ages He has been manifested to put away sin by the sacrifice of Himself" (9:26).

"By this will we have been sanctified through the offering of the body of Jesus Christ once for all" (10:10).

"But He, having offered one sacrifice for sins for all time, SAT DOWN AT THE RIGHT HAND OF GOD" (10:12).

"For by one offering He has perfected for all time those who are sanctified" (10:14).

Again the Jewish believers had a little mix up here because they believed in the sacrifice of Jesus for their sins but they were still holding on to the sacrifices of animals. Even after they got saved by the forgiveness of sins through the death of Jesus, what happened when they sinned again? Is the sacrifice still effectual? If you really believe in the "once for all" perfect, finished work of Christ, it is the way unto maturity. There are many Christians today who are not clear on this, and their consciences can be spooked into not being sure that they are Christians because after their confession of faith they did something wrong. You know how the enemy can get in and work you around. If we would go on to maturity we have to stand in this absolute "once for all." And of course, for those who have broken through, how wonderful it is to rest in His finished work. Even with all our failures, all of our problems, and all of our sins, we can rest in His finished work because it was once for all, never to be undone, never to be repeated.

And interestingly or paradoxically it is when one sees this absolute perfect work of Christ, that we have been made perfect by the sacrifice, that we are freed to press on to perfection. Isn't that interesting? People who press on to perfection through works and strivings and everything they see are on the wrong basis and will eventually run out of gas.

"For by one offering He has perfected for all time those who are sanctified" (10:14). He has already perfected those for all times. That is you and me. Do you believe it? He has already perfected you. Do you believe it? That is the basis for you pressing on to perfection and being made perfect. If you do not believe that, then you think you are attaining to something that you have not gotten to yet. If you understand you have it already, then you just go on to becoming what you already are. There is a lot of difference in those two. So that is the second absolute.

These things are just basic, but I just want to make this point. Sometimes we need to stand upon the word of God in this objective truth and then the Lord can begin to bring us into the maturity that we need.

No Going Back

The third absolute I want to mention from the book of Hebrews is this. There is no going back. A major example in the book of Hebrews is the children of Israel who were in the wilderness and they tried to test the Lord. They said, "Let's go back. Let's appoint other leaders." There is no going back, no going back. Let's look at a couple of verses along that line.

When he talks about the great saints in the school of faith in chapter 11, he is sort of summarizing in the middle of Abraham's testimony, and he has this to say in verse 13-16: "All these died in faith, without receiving the promises, but having seen them and having welcomed them from a distance, and having confessed that they were strangers and exiles on the earth. For those who say such things make it clear that they are seeking a country of their own. And indeed if they had been thinking of that country from which they went out, they would have had opportunity to return. (But there is no return.) But as it is, they desire a better country, that is, a heavenly one. Therefore God is not ashamed to be called their God; for He has prepared a city for them."

Once you get going there is no going back. Some people hang around in the shadows: "Well I am saved, but I am thinking of going back to the world because this saved business is not really turning me on too much." They do not realize that once you have gone through the Red Sea you cannot reopen the Red Sea. If you go back you would drown. There is one way out and there is no going back.

Where are we going? It does not matter where you start, if you go on to maturity you eventually end up outside the camp, and that is what is mentioned in chapter 13:13. Because Jesus is outside the camp He says, "So, let us go out to Him outside the camp, bearing His reproach." Now that has immediate application to those Jewish Christians. The camp was

Judaism. If you are going on to maturity, you have to go outside the camp. Your sufficiency is not in the practice of Judaism; it has got to be in Christ alone. There is no going back now. You have set your course, going toward the Lord, now draw near to Him, and do not go back. You cannot go back. It will not work going back. Staying back is that which makes us fall away.

We read in chapter 3:12 that we have to be careful less the deceitfulness of sin and hardness of heart cause us to fall away from the living God. That is a backward step. It is made even more dangerous when it comes to chapter 6 and it talks about after having tasted of all these things and then falling away. Then there is real trouble. I do not believe you lose your salvation but what he goes on to say is that if you fall away from all the things the Lord has given you and blessed you with—forgiveness, the Holy Spirit, the word of God, and a taste of the life to come, that which replaces all of that encouragement is a sense of dread and a sense of a judgment that is about to fall on you. You cannot go back. If you go back you fall into these kind of shadow lands. Do you know some Christians living in the shadow lands? You say, "Are they Christians?" You can remember the time when they were saved; they asked Jesus to come into their life and they started walking. You can remember that, and you have to say, "Yes, I believe they are truly Christians. I have a witness in my spirit that they really belong to the Lord." But what happened to them? They may have gotten a job and moved somewhere. I do not know what is happening. It is sort of like time stands still. And some of us have experienced that, haven't we? We went away from the Lord for some years, and then we came back. Those five years you were away is like nothing happened. You just wasted five years. There is no going back, and you have to set your mind for that. There is no going back. You cannot go back. What will you do, go back and hide in the world? You will be found. Christians smell different. They will find you out. There is no going back. You have got to press on toward Jesus; you cannot turn back.

That is what the whole matter of the Apostle of our faith is all about. Here again we find this other interesting paradox. Once you make this steely resolve in the cold light of faith that there is no going back, the living way forward seems to open up. Once you cut off your escape route, then God opens the way forward. So these things are important in our stand toward maturity.

A Shaking

The last one I will just mention, and it is a strong word of encouragement, a strong word of exhortation in this book. Here is what we have to face. I hope you can face this. There is going to be a shaking. We have a brother, who every time he speaks now, mentions about the United States and our total naivety. We live in a la-la-la world. Everything is fine; nothing is wrong. This is God's country. We are well protected. What could possibly go wrong? And even though we feel ground tremors, we say no; everything is good. Let's press on with the gospel of prosperity. Let's all get rich and love Jesus and all this kind of stuff. This brother really gets into us, but leaving that aside, the Lord is going to shake this thing up. That means the assembly where you and I are, our own personal lives, and the United States or any other country that you want to name. He has got to shake things up, to shake out the stuff that is shakable. He wants to purify a people. He wants to simplify a people. He wants to focus a people. He has got to shake. It is going to shake. Does that scare you to death?

I remember a dear sister on Long Island. There were different meetings on Long Island for a while, and there was one a ways out on the Island that this sister attended. They happened to be building a nuclear energy plant five miles from her home. They had just bought the home, and then they started building this plant. She was absolutely shaking in her boots; she did not know what to do. This plant did not have a good escape route plan, and after the six billion dollar building was put up it never ran one day. They disassembled it and they strapped the people with an electric bill of ten billion dollars debt because they never did have an escape route.

I remember one time we were talking about it and this lady started crying: "What am I going to do? What am I going to do? If this thing melts down, my children and I are five miles away. What are we going to do?" One of the other sisters who had been patient up to that point said, "I will tell you what I am going to do. If I am over at your house and it melts down and there is no way out, I am going to walk right into that nuclear reactor and get it over with. I am not going to lie around burning for years." And it snapped this girl right out of her fear. I guess she took that resolve. I do not know if she kept her tires pumped up on her bicycle or what but she determined if it happened, she was going to walk toward it; that's it! But it set her free.

That is a silly example, but there is going to be shaking. If you can handle that, then you also find out that there is grace sufficient for any shaking. If you are with the Lord He takes you through the shaking. You will be shaken and I will be shaken; nobody is exempt. You do not get exempt from shaking.

You meet these people who get these squirrelly ideas: "Hey, what you doing?"

"I am retiring and I am going to Panama."

"Panama!" I suppose that is as far away as you think you can be from trouble, but I think it is right in the middle of trouble. But people get ideas of where it is safe. "Montana! That's the place! If everything goes down, move to Montana." No, I just think if we can handle the fact and prepare ourselves, set our minds to understand that there is suffering ahead in these end days, not only because the enemy has something he wants to do and the time is short, but the Lord is going to shake His bride until she is good and ready. That means you and I. Don't be afraid of it. You just walk into the Lord, and then whatever needs to be shaken will be shaken.

JUDGMENT

I live in my own place just like you, feeling safe and secure. When 9-11 came in 2001 in New York City, I lived on Long Island. That was just a little ground tremor; that's all. But I remember our brother Christian Chen and I were in Queens at the time, and in the message that he shared the next Sunday he said, "You know, brothers and sisters, part of the reason that happened is because we do not take seriously that we need to pray that God's kingdom and covering would stay over New York City. Who prays that? We have been negligent and we are under the same judgment as everyone else."

I really saw something in that time. Am I saying anything out of school by saying that New York City is under God's judgment? He mercifully withholds judgment for a season, that people can be saved, that people can come to their senses. He just shakes a little bit to see who will respond, who gets saved, who wakes up. But New York City is under judgment, and if you live there, you have to settle on that fact. You do not know what is going to happen. May I add that the place where you live is under judgment and all the environment around it. You cannot move far enough away from this judgment. The whole thing is under judgment. I do not think you can love America more than I do. I love this country, but this does not mean I have to lie or be blind about it. We deserve judgment, and God is merciful to withhold that judgment.

You should pray for revival, pray that God would spare, revive, restore, bring the church to maturity, but the present things that are happening are not doing it, and I reckon there is going to be shaking. So let's not just be blindsided by that and get knocked out of our tree and lose our cool. You should expect these things and be pressed into the Lord so that when the shaking comes, we are holding onto that one thing that is unshakable, even our Lord Himself. That will get us through whatever we have to get through. How powerful is the word of God to bring us to maturity! If we can realize that the word is speaking to us and we need to stand in the absolute truths presented to us to believe by faith, then the Lord can take us, prepare us, and move us into the reality and maturity that we are longing for these days.

I am very thankful for this brother whoever he was, maybe Barnabas or somebody else, who came along just as the shaking was starting and said, "Okay my dear brothers, it is time to start letting go of things. The day will come if you have not let go you will be devastated."

I wonder what it was like in 71 AD, the year after the destruction. By the mercy of God thousands of Christians left Jerusalem just before the destruction and went to Pella.

Thousands of Jewish Hebrew Christians evidently believed the words of Jesus when He spoke about the shakings that were coming and believed this exhortation. Whatever the circumstances were, they believed and prayed and left in various numbers and troops and went out to this place called Pella which was across the river, and when the shaking came, thousands of Christians were spared. But I wonder what it was like that next year, what kind of traumatic transition they had to go through. I think first of all they were probably humbled by the fact that God even spared their lives. He had to pretty much pull them out, like Lot was pulled out of Sodom and Gomorrah. That is how much those Hebrew Christians loved Jerusalem. God pulled them out and they realized, "We have been so stupid, we have been so blind. Now what do we do? Our whole system is gone. We have no Solomon's porch to meet on. We have no sacrifices that can be offered. There is no more priesthood. There is no more system. What do we do now?" Probably in the trauma somebody said, "I guess we have to follow Jesus only."

I believe the Lord will bring us all to maturity, some the easy way and some through much humiliation. Oh, may we realize that when God gives us a strong word of exhortation, then there is a strong shaking that is soon to come. But heed His word; stand upon His word; cross over; concentrate ourselves according to His word that we may be able to stand in these last days. May the Lord help us. Amen.

THE BETTER WAY

Hebrews 3:1-14—Wherefore, holy brethren, partakers of the heavenly calling, consider the Apostle and High Priest of our confession, Jesus, who is faithful to him that has constituted him, as Moses also in all his house. For he has been counted worthy of greater glory than Moses, by how much he that has built it has more honor than the house. For every house is built by some one; but he who has built all things is God. And Moses indeed was faithful in all his house, as a ministering servant, for a testimony of the things to be spoken after; but Christ, as Son over his house, whose house are we, if indeed we hold fast the boldness and the boast of hope firm to the end. Wherefore, even as says the Holy Spirit, Today if ye will hear his voice, harden not your hearts, as in the provocation, in the day of temptation in the wilderness; where your fathers tempted me, by proving me, and saw my works forty years. Wherefore I was wroth with this generation, and said, They always err in heart; and they have not

*known my ways; so I swore in my wrath, If they
shall enter into my rest. See, brethren, lest there
be in any one of you a wicked heart of unbelief, in
turning away from the living God. But encourage
yourselves each day, as long as it is called Today,
that none of you be hardened by the deceitfulness
of sin. For we are become companions of the
Christ if indeed we hold the beginning of the
assurance firm to the end.*

*Hebrews 4:1—Let us therefore fear, lest, a
promise being left of entering into his rest, any
one of you might seem to have failed of it.*

*Hebrews 4:11—Let us therefore use diligence
to enter into that rest, that no one may fall after
the same example of not hearkening to the word.*

Let us pray:

*Dear heavenly Father, we do commit Thy own
Word back into Thy hands, and ask Thee to bless
it and break it and give to each one of us that we
may be full. We ask in the name of our Lord Jesus.
Amen.*

The second exhortation is found in chapters 3 and 4 of Hebrews. The great theme that is before us is found in 3:1: "Wherefore, holy brethren, partakers of the heavenly calling ..." The children of Israel received a calling from God, but it was an earthly calling. We, who are the redeemed of the Lord, have received a calling from God and it is a heavenly calling because we are a heavenly people of God.

What is a calling? What has God called us into? The calling that comes from God constitutes our vocation. It becomes our life-long occupation. It is something that we must be fully committed to and totally occupied with. A calling will not only show us our destiny, it will also give us direction for that destiny. God has called us with a heavenly calling. We are partakers of a heavenly calling, and the word *partakers* means "sharers." We share that heavenly calling together.

In chapters 3 and 4 of the book of Hebrews we will find three things mentioned that form this heavenly calling. Number one, we are called to be the house of God. "But Christ, as Son over

His house, whose house are we, if indeed we hold fast the boldness and the boast of hope firm to the end" (Hebrews 3:6).

Number two, we are called to be the companions of Christ, and the word "companions" is the same word as the word "partakers" in Hebrews 3:1. "For we are become companions of the Christ if indeed we hold the beginning of the assurance firm to the end" (Hebrews 3:14).

Number three, we are called to enter into His rest. "Let us therefore fear, lest, a promise being left of entering into his rest, any one of you might seem to have failed of it" (Hebrews 4:1).

HOUSE OF GOD

We are called to be the house of God. We are not only being justified, we are not only being glorified, we are not only as many sons whom the Son will lead into glory individually, but we are called corporately to be the house of God. This is our heavenly calling. Can you find any calling more heavenly and more spiritual than this?

It is the eternal desire of God to dwell among men. After He redeemed the children of Israel out of Egypt, He brought them to Mount Sinai where He gave them His Law. He also commanded Moses to build Him a tabernacle because this was to be His dwelling place among the children of Israel. How much better it is today that God does not dwell in a physical tabernacle in order to live among His people. Instead, God has made His people His home; therefore, He dwells directly in and among His own people. He has called us to be His house, His holy habitation, His spiritual house. That is our heavenly calling.

But let us take note of one little word in verse 6—*if.* Whenever you find the word *if*, it means that we are not dealing with this matter objectively as truth. It is objectively true, but when the word *if* is there, we know we are now entering into the realm of subjective experience.

High privilege demands great responsibility—the higher the privilege, the greater the responsibility. We are so privileged to be called the house of God—that God would dwell in our midst, God would find His rest in us, God's heart would be satisfied with us, that God would be loved and worshipped and served by His people. This is a tremendous privilege, but because the privilege is so high the responsibility is very great. That is why the word *if* is there. We are God's house *if*..."

Do not think that the house of God comes automatically—because you are saved, therefore you are the house of God. Not so! One stone, even if it is a living stone, is not a house. These living stones have to be built up together in order to be a house and that is where our responsibility is.

It is true that our Lord Jesus said: "I will build my church upon this rock." It is the Lord Himself who builds the house. He is not only a Son over His house, but He is also the builder of the house. He is going to build the believers together as living stones upon Himself as the foundation to be a holy habitation for God. That is the work that our Lord Jesus will do. But we must remember that He is going to build us up. Unless we are willing to yield ourselves into His hand

and co-operate with Him, He will not be able to build us together in Himself. That is why the word *if* is there—"... whose house are we, if indeed we hold fast the boldness and the boast of hope firm to the end."

What is our hope? Our hope is that one day we will be the finished house of God so that God can dwell among us eternally. God can make us His eternal home and then we will find our eternal home in Him. This is our hope. "Let us hold fast the boldness and the boast of our hope firm to the end." In other words, this is our boast; this is our boldness that one day we will become the completed house of God. Hold fast to that, and do not give it up easily because in the very process of building us together there is much chiseling, cutting, sawing, smoothing, refining, and reducing. In other words, there is much work to be done in our lives which is the cross. Because there is such a working of the cross in our life, sometimes we get disappointed, or discouraged, or we faint and want to draw back or flee away. Therefore, we refuse to co-operate and we give up our hope. And if we do, then the Lord is not able to build us into His house or build us together. That is the why the word *if* is there.

Dear brothers and sisters, how can we hold fast the boldness and the boast of hope to the end? Here is the secret: "Christ in you, the hope of glory." In other words, it is because Christ is in you. As a matter of fact, Christ is not taking you and me as the building blocks of the house; He is actually taking Himself in you and me to build up the house of God. The reason you and I have to be eliminated is that He may be increased and we be decreased in order that the house may be built. Thank God, "Christ in you the hope of glory." In me, that is in my flesh there is no good. If it depends upon me, not only will I fail, but God will have to give up. Thank God, it does not depend on me! It depends on the Christ in me and because He is in me, He is the hope of glory. One day, that house will be built and this is our heavenly calling.

COMPANIONS OF CHRIST

We are companions or active partners of Christ. We are to be full partners; not as some people say "sleeping partners"—which means we are partners but not active at all. We are to be actively engaged together in the business Christ came to earth to do.

We like to share with Christ in having our sins forgiven and in the gift of eternal life. In other words, we like to share with Christ in what we call common salvation or initial salvation. But how many brothers and sisters are willing to be living partners with Christ in His business and in the very purpose that Christ came to fulfill?

The reason Christ came into the world is to build His house in order that He may have a body and when that body is fully grown, He may have His bride. Now that is the business that Christ is engaged with. Are we actively involved in that business?

The apostle Paul said: "I rejoice in suffering for you because I am filling up the affliction of Christ concerning His body" (see Colossians 1:24). Are we just interested in our own interest? Are we interested only in going to heaven? Of course, we are interested, but has that become our sole interest? Or are we taken up with the interest of Christ? Are we just concerned with our welfare or are we concerned with the welfare of God? If we are concerned with the welfare of God, then we become active partners with Christ and companions of Christ. One day, those who accompany Christ on earth today will become His companions when He will be crowned and receive His bride.

In Psalm 45, which is a prophecy of the marriage of the king and the queen, it is also a prophecy concerning the union of Christ and His church. God has anointed Him with the oil of gladness above His companions. This tells us that there will be companions there, but let us remember that only those who follow the Lamb wheresoever He goes will become His companions at His marriage feast. We need to hold fast the assurance of our hope firm to the end. Again the word *if* is there; it is a great responsibility.

ENTERING INTO HIS REST

The third thing spoken of in the heavenly calling is this matter of entering into His rest. When the children of Israel were in Egypt there

The Better Way

was no rest because they were slaves and were put in hard labor. They were in a fiery furnace. They were not even going to be allowed to live; the whole race was to be eliminated. BUT GOD— delivered them out of Egypt with the purpose of leading them into Canaan which meant rest for them. God wanted to lead them into rest that they might dwell in the land in safety and in peace, enjoying the land that was flowing with milk and honey. This was God's purpose concerning His people.

While God was leading them to Canaan, unfortunately, even though He proved Himself to them many times that He was faithful, that He was true to His Word, that there was nothing too hard for Him, and that He loved them, yet this people rebelled in their hearts. They hardened their hearts toward God and refused to believe His Word. They even questioned God's love and faithfulness. Therefore, even though God endured them and suffered long with them, finally, when they arrived at Kadesh-Barnea, that was the end. There came a point when God said: "Because this generation erred in their hearts, they do not know My ways, and they have provoked Me again and again and again, this generation cannot enter into My rest."

The Work is Finished

We have a promise of entering into God's rest. What is rest? And how do we enter into His rest? We cannot rest if the work is not finished, but when the work is finished, then we can rest.

God used six days to repair the earth, and on the seventh day He rested from His work, because the work was done. Even though man was created on the sixth day, actually the first day that man lived was the seventh day. In other words, it was God's purpose that man was to be created on the sixth day and immediately enter into God's rest. But unfortunately, man sinned, and he not only lost that rest in God, but God lost His rest.

Immediately after man sinned, God came to the garden to seek and to find the lost: "Adam, where are you?" God began to work and that is the reason the Lord Jesus spoke to the Pharisees as He did after He healed on the Sabbath day. The Pharisees said: "The Sabbath day is a day of rest; you should not heal anybody." The Lord said, "My Father works until now and I work." In other words, where there is sin there is no rest; therefore, God had no rest. He has to work until the work is done; then He will rest. Thank God, on Calvary's cross the last word that our Lord Jesus shouted in victory was: "It is finished!" The work is done and because the work was done on Calvary's cross, today our Lord Jesus sits at the right hand of God because the work is done. The work of redemption is finished; therefore, we are called to enter into His rest. We are to rest in His rest, which means we are to rest in the finished work of Christ.

Why is it that we are so restless? When the children of Israel were in the wilderness, they were restless. That whole picture is of a person who is living according to the flesh. We are born of the Spirit, and yet daily we still live according to the flesh, even though we try to live according to the good flesh and not the bad. Flesh is not all bad; there is the good flesh and the bad flesh. The bad flesh commits sin and the good flesh tries to please God or appease God or bribe God. As long as we are trying to live in the flesh, we become restless. As a result of this, we strive, we struggle, we strain, we stretch, and we keep trying. But in me, that is in my flesh, there is no good. Then we begin to murmur, or doubt, or lose heart, and begin to distrust God. Then we find ourselves in the wilderness where there is no rest.

Our rest is in Christ, who is Canaan to us, and His finished work. The reason we do not have rest is because we do not believe. We believe in ourselves more than we believe in Him and what He has done for us. The moment we enter into the finished work of Christ our soul enters into rest. In Matthew 11:28 the Lord Jesus said, "Come to me, all ye who labor and are heavy laden and I will give you rest."

When we were in sins and transgressions, we had no rest and the Lord said: "Come unto Me; just come to Me all you who labor and are heavy laden, and I will give you rest. I will take away your burden and the load you are carrying, because I have already taken it upon Myself when I was on the cross." In *Pilgrim's Progress,* that pilgrim fled from the city of destruction and came to the cross, and as he looked at the cross the burden on his back rolled away.

Take My Yoke

Thank God, we who believe in the Lord Jesus have that rest in our spirit. But the Lord said there is another rest: "Take my yoke upon you, and learn from me; for I am meek and lowly in heart; and ye shall find rest to your souls" (Matthew 11:29).

Thank God, when we come to the Lord Jesus with heavy burdens, He gives us rest in the spirit and it is there forever. But unfortunately, oftentimes we are still in the wilderness, and our soul is still restless because we do not take His yoke upon us.

What is the yoke of Christ? It is the will of God. The Lord Jesus said: "Lo, I come to do Your will." The Lord took upon Himself the will of God as His yoke to control and guide Him. He took it willingly, voluntarily, happily, joyfully, and victoriously. When He put that yoke upon Himself, He was meek and lowly in heart. There was no resistance or fighting against the Father's will: "Not My will, but Your will be done." He was selfless, and He yielded Himself completely to the Father. He accomplished the will of God!

This is why He can say, "Take My yoke upon you and learn from Me." This yoke has two holes. On the one side is the Lord Jesus and He yokes us to the other side, because we are like the unbroken oxen or horse. He is going to break us by yoking us with the One who has been broken, who is always broken, and when He puts us with Christ in His field, may we learn of Him. Look at Him! When you are restless, look at Him. When you rebel, look at Him. When you feel it is too hard, look at Him.

When we do this, we will find rest in our soul because we enter into the good of His finished work. This is our calling—into His rest.

I am just explaining it spiritually. Actually, in reading this more closely, we see that rest here is His rest, and not our rest. When we learn of Him, we do enter into rest in our soul, but the whole point here is His rest. We have the promise of entering into His rest which means that when everything He wants to do is done, then He will rest. That happens during the millennial kingdom, and at that time He will have His bride. At that time He will rest in His own rest and we will rest with Him. So spiritually, the rest is something we should experience daily, even today, but dispensationally it is a promise that is before us, and if we use diligence we will enter into His rest. We will reign and rule with Christ for a thousand years.

These three things compose our heavenly calling. We are called to be the house of God, but in order to be the house of God experientially and not just positionally, we have to yield ourselves to His hand and let Him build us. We are called to be the companions of Christ, and if we want to be His companions, then we have to be actively engaged in His business. We are called to enter into His rest but to do so we have to take His yoke upon us. If we do that, one day we shall rest in His rest in the millennial kingdom.

ENCOURAGEMENT

This is the theme that is before us. Can you think of anything greater than these things? This is the heavenly calling. With such a heavenly calling, the writer wants to encourage us. He says: "Having this before us what should we do?"

Consider

"Consider the Apostle and High Priest of our confession, Jesus." The English word *consider* comes from the Latin word which is the word for "star" and the root of that word is "astronomer." He looks at the star; he considers, contemplates, gazes patiently, persistently, with concentration. He gazes at the stars and tries to discover the stars in the sky. That is the meaning of the word *consider*. Therefore in the spiritual realm it means that we should gaze upon the Lord Jesus, fix our gaze upon Him, contemplate Him, think about Him, ponder over Him, and concentrate our thought in Him.

We are to consider Him as the Apostle of our confession. The Lord Jesus is the Apostle of our confession. An apostle is one who is sent on a mission. The Lord Jesus is God's Apostle, and He was sent on a mission to build the house of God.

Moses was an apostle to the children of Israel, and he was called to build God a house, a tabernacle so that God might dwell among His people. And Moses was faithful in all His house. But here we are told that the Lord Jesus is God's Apostle, not only to the children of Israel, but to the whole world. He is to gather out of every nation, every tongue, and every tribe a people to be built together into the house of God. He is not only the builder; He is also the owner of the house. How much greater is He than Moses!

The Lord calls us, justifies us, glorifies us in order to build us together to be His house. He says, "I will build my house upon this rock (that is Himself as the foundation), and the gates of Hades shall not prevail against it" (see Matthew 16:18). There is a spiritual conflict going on over the building, but thank God, the victory is already won and the gates of Hades shall not prevail against it. In other words, He will have His house. He has overcome all the forces of His enemy on Calvary's cross. He has delivered us out of the power of darkness and has translated us into the kingdom of the Son of God's love. He has done everything, He has provided everything and He is able to save us to the uttermost. He is a High Priest, ministering to us day by day in heaven that He may save us to the uttermost. Let us consider Him, and even though it may seem impossible with us, nothing is impossible with Him. That is how our boast and boldness are kept to the end. Consider Him because it is not something you and I can do. All work is done by Him, our Apostle; all we need do is hand ourselves over to Him and let Him do it. Are we willing to do that?

Consider Jesus, the Apostle of our confession. He has already entered behind the veil as the forerunner. There is a Man in heaven sitting at the right hand of God and that Man is beckoning us to heaven. That gives us hope. He has opened the way for us and is calling us to join Him. This Son is to lead many sons into glory, and He is determined to build us together that the gates of Hades shall not prevail against it. He will do it. Are we willing to trust Him?

Encourage One Another

"But encourage yourselves each day, as long as it is called Today, that none of you be hardened by the deceitfulness of sin" (Hebrews 3:13).

First, let us consider Jesus and then let us encourage one another. Do not consider your brothers and sisters first. If you consider your brothers and sisters first before you consider Christ, all you will receive is the weakness and the faults of your brothers and sisters. A brother once said: "I have considered that brother with a microscope." We need to consider our brothers and sisters with a telescope. However, let us consider Jesus, and if we use a microscope that is fine. But after we have considered Him, then we are to encourage one another because we are to be the house of God. It is not a matter of you and Him alone; it is a matter of you and Him and the brothers and sisters. Do not think of your own spirituality alone. Think of your brothers and sisters. Let us encourage our brothers and sisters because if they should fail the house will be delayed. It takes all of us together to build up the house and to be companions of Christ. Christ does not have just one companion; He has many.

Therefore, we need to encourage one another daily, as long as it is today. Thank God, today is the day that God has made. Let us rejoice in it. I always thank God for today. Oftentimes I tell God, "Lord, I thank You that You have given me another day—a day of opportunity." As long as there is a day which is called today, there is hope. The Spirit of God still has a chance to work and we still have a chance to let Him work. So as long as it is today, let us encourage one another daily, lest any one should fail.

Let Us Fear

"Let us therefore fear, lest, a promise being left of entering into his rest, any one of you might seem to have failed of it" (Hebrews 4:1).

Holy fear is an important ingredient in love. It is true that in I John it says, "Perfect love casts out fear;" but the fear there means the fear of punishment and perfect love casts out that kind of fear. But the Scripture says, "The fear of the Lord is the beginning of wisdom." In other words, there is a holy fear which is an important ingredient in love. Now if we love a person are we fearful? We are not afraid of being punished, but we are fearful lest we displease him. We want to please him so much that we are in fear, and that is a kind of holy fear.

Today, people are so careless, so loose. Sometimes our relationship with the Lord is too intimate. Of course, in one sense we cannot be too intimate with the Lord. But in another sense, sometimes it is a little bit unholy because of a lack of fear, as if we can do anything we want to and it does not matter. After all, He loves us, so what matters? Do we have that holy fear?—the fear that we may miss out; we may miss His purpose; we may displease Him; we may fail Him. It is nothing if we fail, but to fail Him—that makes a great difference. Are we afraid of that?

Diligence

"Let us therefore use diligence to enter into that rest" (Hebrews 4:11). Now, is that not a contradiction? On one hand, we are to enter into rest, but on the other hand, we are to exercise diligence and that means using some energy which is not resting. Wherein is that diligence to enter into that rest? We find it in the following verses: "The word of God is sharper than a two-edged sword" (v. 12). It penetrates, it cuts asunder, it divides the bone and marrow, the spirit and the soul, and it reveals the intents and thoughts of the heart for there is nothing that is not naked and laid bare before His eyes. In other words, "using diligence to enter into His rest" simply means to exercise our will to lie on the altar as a living sacrifice. Do not get off; do not struggle. Let the Priest, the Holy Spirit, use the knife, the living word of God, to divide our soul and spirit, and when our soul is divided from our spirit we enter into His rest. It is not our working but it is using diligence to lay there and not move. That is where the diligence is.

WARNINGS

Unbelief

We have looked at the encouragements, now we come to the warnings. We find that the warnings are being given because of the greatness of these things. "See brethren, lest there be in any one of you a wicked heart of unbelief in turning away from the living God" (Hebrews 3:12). Remember, these words are spoken to believers. This wicked heart of unbelief can happen to a believer. Take careful note of this. The example is used of the children of Israel (Psalm 95), who were delivered out of Egypt and then provoked the Lord in the wilderness. They did not believe in Him, they tested Him, they proved Him, they erred in heart, and they did not know His way. This happened to the delivered children of Israel, and thus this warning is to believers—brethren: "See brethren, be careful brethren, lest there be in any one of you a wicked heart of unbelief." "If any one thinks that he can stand, let him be careful lest he fall" (see I Corinthians 10:12).

Our relationship with the Lord is a matter of the heart. God has created us with a heart, and with this heart we are to fellowship with God in faith and in love. But unfortunately, this heart became a heart of stone, a stony heart through the deceitfulness of sin. Sin has deceived us and made our hearts as hard as stone; it is very deceitful. We recall how the serpent tempted Eve and how deceitful he was. It seems that the serpent suggested something that was very insignificant; just a matter of eating a fruit. What is the big issue with eating a fruit? He suggested that they would be wise, they would be clever, they would be like God—so many promises.

Sin is very deceitful. When sin comes, it deceives people. It tries to lure people into thinking there is so much pleasure in it, but it is a lie. It offers so much, as if it will satisfy you, and sometimes it seems so insignificant, such a small thing. Maybe it is just a little worldliness, a little pride, or a little jealously. It is something insignificant, but if you yield to it that sin begins to loom bigger and bigger until you are under the dominion of it, and your heart becomes hard as stone towards God. You are not able to hear Him anymore. You will not be moved by His voice anymore, and that is what the human heart had become. There was no fellowship between man and God because the heart was stony.

But thank God, when we are convicted by the Holy Spirit and we come to the Lord Jesus, God takes away our stony heart and gives us a heart of flesh (see Ezekiel 36:26). A heart of flesh simply means that it is a living heart, a tender heart, a feeling heart, a heart that can be touched and moved by God, and can hear His voice. Our heart is the ear that hears Him, the eyes that see Him, and the capacity to receive His communication.

It is possible, even with this heart of flesh, not to hear His voice today, and tomorrow another today, and tomorrow another today. If we do not hear His voice now while the Spirit of God is speaking to us, it may become hardened. We may have a heart of flesh and He is able to speak to us, but do we listen? If we do not listen, if we do not obey, if we do not cooperate, our heart gets hardened a little bit, and the next day if we do not listen, it gets hardened further. Finally, we may so harden our heart that it becomes a wicked heart of unbelief. We just will not believe; therefore, we do not mix faith with His word, we do not yield to His voice. The result is that we turn away from the living God.

Dear brothers and sisters, high is our privilege! Great is our responsibility! That is the reason we have to encourage one another lest someone among us gets deceived by sin. In the beginning it may be a very small, insignificant thing. It may not be a very blatant sin. It may be something very small and hidden, but when the Holy Spirit speaks to our heart, do we yield to Him? Do we believe in God's Word? Do we let God's word cut off that sin? If we harden our heart, it will get harder and harder and harder until it becomes a wicked heart of unbelief. May the Lord deliver us from such a wicked heart of unbelief. Verse 13 says, "... that none of you be hardened by the deceitfulness of sins."

COME SHORT

"Let us therefore fear, lest a promise being left of entering into his rest, any one of you might seem to have failed of it" (Hebrews 4:1). You failed it; that means, "come short of it." It is God's will that we should enter into His rest today and in the millennium to come; but if we fail it, if we fall short of it, we cannot blame Him. The first generation children of Israel failed in the wilderness. They did not enter into Canaan because of their unbelief, but thank God, there were Joshua and Caleb. They had a more excellent spirit. They believed in God and believed in His Word, and they entered into the Promised Land.

May we not be like those who failed in the wilderness, who came short of God's purpose, but may we be like Caleb and Joshua, mingling faith with the Word we hear that we may enter into His rest. "That no one may fall after the same example of not hearkening to the word" (Hebrews 4:11); that we will not fall by the wayside, that we may continue on until we enter into His rest.

Thank God, He has not only put before us a tremendous calling, a heavenly calling, but He has made every provision for us to make it. He is the Apostle and the High Priest of our confession and we are to encourage one another. Every provision is there. Let us make use of His provision and not harden our hearts through the deceitfulness of sin and develop a wicked heart of unbelief that will cause us to fall and fail and come short of the purpose of God.

Shall we pray:

Dear heavenly Father, how we do praise and thank Thee that Thou hast called us with a heavenly calling, and what a calling it is! Thou wants us to be Thy house, Thy companion, and into Thy rest. Oh Father, we just desire it very much, and we do praise and thank Thee that Thou dost call us to consider Jesus, the Apostle and High Priest of our confession, and Thou dost also encourage us to encourage and exhort one another daily as it is today, that we, by Thy grace, may make it. Oh our Father, do be merciful to us, that none of us will fall by the wayside, but we may all enter into that rest that Thou hast provided for us. And we praise and worship Thee in the name of our Lord Jesus. Amen.

JESUS AS HIGH PRIEST

Hebrews 2-3:1—For this reason we must pay much closer attention to what we have heard, so that we do not drift away from it. For if the word spoken through angels proved unalterable, and every transgression and disobedience received a just penalty, how will we escape if we neglect so great a salvation? After it was at the first spoken through the Lord, it was confirmed to us by those who heard, God also testifying with them, both by signs and wonders and by various miracles and by gifts of the Holy Spirit according to His own will. For He did not subject to angels the world to come, concerning which we are speaking. But one has testified somewhere, saying,

What is man, that You remember him? Or the son of man, that You are concerned about him? You have made him for a little while lower than the angels; You have crowned him with glory and honor, and have appointed him over the works of Your hands; You have put all things in subjection under his feet.

For in subjecting all things to him, He left nothing that is not subject to him. But now we do not yet see all things subjected to him. But we do see [Jesus] who was made for a little while lower than the angels, namely, Jesus, because of the suffering of death crowned with glory and honor, so that by the grace of God He might taste death for everyone. For it was fitting for Him, for whom are all things, and through whom are all things, in bringing many sons to glory, to perfect the author of their salvation through sufferings. For both He who sanctifies and those who are sanctified are all from one Father; for which reason He is not ashamed to call them brethren, saying,

I will proclaim Your name to My brethren, in the midst of the congregation I will sing Your praise.

And again, I will put My trust in Him.

And again, Behold, I and the children whom God has given Me.

Since then the children share in flesh and blood, He Himself likewise also partook of the same, so that through death He might render powerless him who had the power of death, that is, the devil, and might free those who through fear of death were subject to slavery all their lives. For assuredly He does not give help to angels, but He gives help to the descendant of Abraham. Therefore, He had to be made like His brethren in all things, so that He might become a merciful and faithful high priest in things pertaining to God, to make propitiation for the sins of the people. For since He Himself was tempted in that which He has suffered, He is able to come to the aid of those who are tempted.

Therefore, holy brethren, partakers of a heavenly calling, consider Jesus, the Apostle and High Priest of our confession.

Hebrews 12:25-29—See to it that you do not refuse Him who is speaking. For if those did not escape when they refused him who warned on earth, much less will we escape who turn away from Him who warns from heaven. And His voice shook the earth then, but now He has promised, saying, YET ONCE MORE I WILL SHAKE NOT ONLY THE EARTH, BUT ALSO THE HEAVEN. This expression, "Yet once more," denotes the removing of those things which can be shaken, as of created things, so that those things which cannot be shaken may remain. Therefore, since we receive a kingdom which cannot be shaken, let us [have grace] by which we may offer to God an acceptable service with reverence and awe; for our God is a consuming fire.

Hebrews 13:22—But I urge you, brethren, bear with this word of exhortation, for I have written to you briefly.

Our Father, as we come to You, we are so thankful for Your precious word before us. We know that whoever that apostolic writer was he was obviously inspired of the Holy Spirit to pen these words direct from heaven. Even these warnings were not the prophecies of men but indeed the warnings from heaven. And so as we gather together before Your word we want to hear Your voice beyond the voice of the speaker. We pray that the Holy Spirit would speak to our hearts and open up our understanding with a Spirit of wisdom and revelation in the knowledge of Jesus Christ that we may enter in and press on to maturity which is the only way forward. We thank You, Lord, that You have gathered us for such a time to consider weighty matters, and we ask for the help of the Holy Spirit in speaking and receiving and understanding and in obeying. Lord, we come to You in the precious and blessed name of our Lord Jesus Christ. Amen.

For anybody who has studied the book of Hebrews you know that this is a mature book. It is a book of strong exhortation. There is a phrase in Hebrews 6 that refers to strong exhortation, strong encouragement, and surely this whole letter to the Hebrews is such a word of strong encouragement. And the Lord is always faithful to send a strong word of encouragement before any great shaking. These Jewish Christians were Christians, but only half-way home; they were not all the way through. They were Christians living somewhat in the shadow of the Jewish traditions and they were being warned from heaven: "Let go; let go and lay hold of Jesus as your all-sufficiency because a shaking will come, and if you are holding onto anything shakable you will suffer. Hold on to the Lord; hold on to the Lord. And of course we know, historically, exactly what this prophet said came to pass. What a strong word of exhortation!

You would be interested to know that every time this word *exhortation* or *encouragement* is used it is actually "warning, encouragement, and exhortation." These three words are all the same word, and it is always the word *Paraclete*, that same word we have for the Holy Spirit which means "to be called alongside." It is as if the writer is saying, "I give you a word of a strong coming alongside of God to you." That is what encouragement is. When one comes along our side, even as the Holy Spirit who has become our Paraclete, He comforts us. And in the original King James English back in those days, *comfort* meant "to strengthen," coming from that word *fort* to "be fortified." So the first meaning for *your comforter* was actually "your strengthener" and secondarily, He is the One who gives you comfort and succor and mercy when you have need. And we find here that the word of God is also such a strengthener. We need a faith that is strong and able to stand through the test of the last days, and so we have this precious word.

The first night I simply tried to say by way of introduction that this is a book of strong exhortation. It exhorts the saints to leave behind those shadows and press on into maturity, to settle four issues that forever marked those who have moved on to maturity. The first one is to settle it: Jesus is God. He is not just a good man, not just a Savior, Son of God; He is God, the Son of God. And when somebody finally deals with this, as these Jewish Christians sometimes were hesitant to do, when they recognized the divinity of the Lord Jesus, there was a freedom to move on and take Him as their all-sufficiency.

The second issue that needed to be settled was His sacrifice, His atonement, His perfect work. His finished work was one time for all. Once it was done it does not need to be repeated. It covers every sin that you have committed and will commit. It is once for all. You do not go back; you do not sacrifice again. Jesus did it one time, and we need to settle on that. Otherwise, Christians who have been forgiven fall into a condemnation: "What do I do now? I have sinned again since believing in Jesus." That same finished work is still effective for us all through our lives by His grace and mercy. This is an issue that needs to be settled in our hearts because it is that issue that usually brings one to that great moment of assurance of their salvation. And the enemy can no longer convince them they are not saved because they know that that work ever pleads our cause.

The third thing that we have to face is that once you have set out there is no going back. The writer to the Hebrews makes this clear with his example of the children in the wilderness who wandered. There is only one way forward and it is into the land of Canaan. You cannot go back. The Red Sea will not reopen and let you go back. There is one way forward; it is the way of the Lord. It is the way that is seen so faithfully in Abraham when he said in Hebrews that he could have gone back if he wanted to but he never wanted to because he sought a better country, even a heavenly home. And so must we press forward. There is no going back. Don't let the enemy talk you into going back into the world. You will never find a home there again. It is only forward that we can go.

The fourth issue that maturity causes us to settle is that there is coming a shaking, and we will be shaken. Much of the outward things— created things, our comfort, our position, the things we have relied upon perhaps way too much—may be shaken right away from us. Facing that fact we need to ask the Lord to help us let go of those things that we might press on and gain His best even through a time of shaking. We read in chapter 12 that even during the time of shaking there were some who were victorious, and they were able to have grace and serve one another in a time of shaking. That is an overcomer!

In our second session we tried to show by the thirteen convincing references in the book of Hebrews that Jesus is and has opened the better way. This word is used by our writer some thirteen times, some people believe fifteen. The word *superior* is also used there. In any case the emphasis is on the fact that Jesus has opened a better way. Whatever was good in the system of Judaism has been made obsolete because Jesus brought in the better way. It was a better sacrifice with a better tabernacle, with a better calling, with a better priesthood, with better promises, with better blood—better, better, better! He has brought in the better way. He has inaugurated this better way, and even more precious than that, Jesus Himself is God's best, not comparatively better; He *is* God's best.

I wish I had a deeper voice and could read this book a little bit more august, a little more threateningly, that we might feel the ground tremor when we read the words because these words are words of tremor, the words that speak of dire circumstances and warnings ahead, announcing persecution that is sure. But stronger than the words of warning come great encouragement, great and precious promises, great rewards promised to us, and a better portion all the way through. Which voice do we listen to? All of this is part of that great encouragement.

This pressing on to maturity, however you read it in the book of Hebrews, is a very daunting thing. It is a fearful thing frankly as we read there at the end of chapter 12. We serve

God with reverence and awe in the light of the truth of His word. These things are grave.

We know that He is our Savior. We read at the very beginning of this book in chapter 1:3 this wonderful gospel reality which all of us as believers have laid hold of: "When He had made purification of sins, He sat down at the right hand of the Majesty on high, having become as much better than the angels, as He has inherited a more excellent name than they."

How wonderful that probably everybody in this room has seen Jesus who has gone to Calvary for you, that He died for your sins, was raised again, and is seated in glory at the right hand of the Majesty, and you have taken Him as your Savior. What a wonderful place that is!

But in this matter of pressing on to maturity, how do we do this? How do we get started? And that is what I want to share now.

A MAN IN GLORY

It is not in man to direct his steps, nor even to know how to enter into this pressing on to maturity. As much as we may have read the comparisons and all such things, how do we get started? The Lord has provided in His wisdom the way, and our exhorter here, this great man, has shown us the way into pressing on to maturity. And what is that way? In a word, it is to look up. Your heavenly calling is to look up. And the first thing he does here in chapter 2 is have us look up, to look into heaven and see the greatest surprise of heaven. All the angels, the twenty-four elders, the cherubim surrounding the throne are all surprised by Someone who is in heaven. Who is that? There is a Man in the glory! That is a great surprise. Now for you and me it may be la la la because you have heard it before, but in heaven they stand in awe. How did a Man ever make it through to glory, completely transformed, completely glorious, having gone down to earth as a Man, having gone through the severest tests of history, having suffered, having been trodden on and tried, yet He lived a sinless life and then He died for others? Now He is risen and He is at the right hand of the Majesty. There is a Man in the glory! This is how it all opens. We are looking around at man's purpose but we do not see anybody until we can say, "But we see Jesus." There is a Man in the glory! What a surprise! What a praise! And yet wait; there is more than that. When you continue to look into heaven you see the Father's glorious plan.

MANY SONS TO GLORY

It says in Hebrews 2:10: "For it was fitting for Him, for whom are all things, and through whom are all things (the Father), in bringing many sons to glory, to perfect the author of their salvation through sufferings."

We see something glorious. The Father has had a plan since the beginning of time and here it is. His desire is to bring many sons to glory, and so He took His Son who came down and suffered in order to bring many sons to glory. Wait just a minute. Look up there in heaven just another minute and see: that is you! Have you ever seen yourself in the glory? Oh, you think, "That is not me. That is the apostle Paul and Peter and some of those guys." But no, it says here in this gospel that is proclaimed, He is bringing many sons to glory and that is the reason He came down and suffered for our sake. But if you look up there you will see yourself in the glory. That changes a lot of things. What a wonderful thought that is! But you are saying the same thing that the readers who read this said, "No, no this cannot be me." So the writer goes on quickly to say: "Therefore, He is not ashamed to call you 'my brother.'"

You can say, "I am not worthy to be Jesus' brother," but Jesus says, "I do not care about worthiness; by grace you are worthy." He is not ashamed. Look at us. We are ashamed of ourselves half the time. At least we are ashamed of our children most of the time, and when we are in the light of God, we are ashamed of our own actions. And yet here is a God who in light of glory says, "I am not ashamed of you. Furthermore I am going to prove it. I am going to descend and come in among you while you are worshiping and join in the worship of our Father together with you." All of this because of that vision there in the glory. It is only a heavenly vision of the glorious Son and your glorious destiny that will ever bring you into pressing on to maturity. All the words of exhortation will not get you on the road. All the promises set before you like a carrot will not get you very far. All the warnings, all the rewards, all those things stacked up will not get you on the road to pressing on to maturity. But if you can just see the Christ of glory one nana second, one flash of lighting's worth, and see yourself in God's plan in that glory, it will change your whole life.

Someone asked me, "How can you ever pursue God's best? How can you ever let go of earthly things? How can you ever stop living in the shadows and live in that simplicity of life of pursuing the best things and pursuing the Lord alone? I will tell you how—to see Him in the glory, then see yourself in the glory, and watch what goes stripping away.

"Has thou seen Him, heard Him, known Him? Is not thine a captive heart?" What is the basis of that captivity? Are you warned into it? Has someone sort of strong-armed you into it? Well, of course not! It is one moment beholding Him in glory.

Now I just want to make this note, and it is all part of the same revelation of our Lord Jesus Christ. There are many who have seen Him as that One who did the finished work in a perfect way and now sits at the right hand of the Father, but they actually have not seen the Christ of glory. And to understand His high priestly work, to understand His apostolic work among us today, you must see the Christ of glory. There is a Man in the glory. *There is a Man in the glory!* If you do not catch the significance of that, then how do we press forward?

THERE IS A MAN IN THE GLORY!

This is part of our heavenly vision. But our heavenly vision is not just a vision of the glorified Man up there, the Son of Man, even Jesus; the heavenly vision is seeing ourselves in there somehow. When you see yourself in glory as God purposed you to be (I am not saying you are going to see yourself with a halo, angel wings, nice and slim, a white beard), when you see the Christ of glory, and you see yourself in the Christ of glory, your life changes. What could be simpler? In one second your motives begin to be changed. You get spoiled to things you once thought were important and they are no longer that important to you. Your sense of service is no longer "I have got to go to that meeting today. I have got to speak, so I had better come up with something. Or I have got to teach the kids, those crumby kids, I would like to smack them around." No, you find whatever your level of service is, whatever the Lord has called you to do, there is glory in it. There is a very important reason why you are doing it. Service is glorious. Your calling is heavenly; it is glorious. Glory is a tremendous thing. It just lifts all of that which is mundane and all of that which is earthy in the church and in your Christian life. And you realize when you go before the Lord in the morning and read the word, it is a moment of glory. We need to be refreshed in this even for those who have seen these things. How quickly they slip away. Our whole lives are changed in a moment of glory.

So Paul only saw a flash but it changed his whole life. And Isaiah only saw a moment and it changed his whole life. And Job only saw a moment but it changed his whole life. And Abraham only saw a moment and it changed his whole life. Abraham walked on higher ground, he had higher pursuits, and he learned how to walk in a higher way. His family became more important, what he did became more important, the victories were more important, and what he prayed and asked for became more important because he saw himself in the glory.

CONSIDER JESUS

So the writer very simply says, "Therefore, holy brethren, partakers of the heavenly calling, consider Jesus." What our dear brother is suggesting is whether you have seen this Christ of glory or not, if you will fasten your eyes upon Jesus and even get on your knees and fasten your eyes upon Jesus, the Apostle and High Priest of our confession, and ask Him, "Lord, I live such a mundane life. I am held down by so many earthly things; even my service to You is earthbound, and my mind and its working is so natural. Could I just see a moment of glory and see what the end is and what it is all about, and why I have been saved." If you just get there with an honest heart, there is a Spirit that sends wisdom and revelation in the knowledge of Jesus Christ, a Spirit that has been given to the church for those who seek and are hungry. If you do not care, you get nothing. If you are just going to glide, you will not see either the Christ in glory or yourself in glory. But for those who see, it is a pressing on to maturity.

"Consider..." This English word is much too weak. Will you behold Jesus? Will you gaze on Him? Will you consider Him thoroughly? That is the closest to the Greek that I have been able to find. Consider Him thoroughly until some light dawns. This whole business about Jesus is not something dead, it is not just something theological, but there is something living. There is a Man in the glory. The angels see it. They are all a flutter. It would be a shame if we who are destined to be many sons in glory do not even see what we are about. We do not even see the destination and end because we have not seen this wondrous sight.

HEAVENLY VISION

Perhaps we beat a dead horse by saying we need heavenly vision, but honestly, when you see the lives of people, you can almost see those who have caught on to something. It does not matter how rough you are. It does not matter how sorely tempted. It does not matter whether you came out of the gutter. It does not matter whether your education was high or low. None of that stuff matters. The Lord has saved and shown His glory to some very coarse individuals, but my, what a transformation began in their lives! When you think of a guy like D. L. Moody who could hardly read and write when the Lord captured him, and yet his heart was so full by the end of his days that he could just stand up in an auditorium and people would get saved. It does not take an education, it does not take some kind of special nobility, it does not matter whether you are rough or smooth, when you see the Christ of glory, there is something that changes in your life, there is something that hooks into your heart, and it begins to pull you toward maturity and toward the Lord. What a wondrous process this is!

How could we ever press on to maturity? We hardly know the way. We do not know what we are doing, but when we are so struck by this heavenly vision, we start on the way even when we do not want to be on the way. And it is true, a vision of glory does undo you. It is an undoing, but would you rather be undone by glory or undone by this world shaking? If we are undone by glory and the Lord releases those idols that we have held on to until we saw Him, heard Him, knew Him, then whatever shaking comes, He is more than adequate for you because you have held on to that which is best. So if we need to be undone by glory, then we need to be undone by glory. And may our assemblies be undone with a good shaking and then a seeing of glory, and we as individuals as well. This is an upward way.

BUT WE SEE JESUS

What does "partakers of the heavenly calling" mean? It is hard to define. There are some translations that say, "Our calling up to heaven." That is not it. This is partakers of a heavenly calling. If you see the Man in the glory and you see yourself in the glory, you find you are already a partaker. There is something causing you to rise, and there is something renewing your mind. And if you consecrate yourself and say, "Oh Lord, I have seen something I do not even understand, but I want to live on that higher plane," the Lord is so gracious. He lays hold of us and we find a wonderful thing.

Chapter 2 opens up with that wonderful part of Psalm 8: "What is man that Thou are mindful of him? You made Him a little lower than the angels; You crowned Him with dominion and brought all things in subjection to Him." And then the writer says, "We do not see that yet." If you could take all the failures of mankind in falling short of the glory of God, and add to that all the failure of the churches and the assemblies in falling short of the glorious church, and add to that our own personal lives of weakness and frailty and failure, you can write over the top of it, "But we see Jesus," because the whole thing is impossible. But when you see the Man in glory, you have suddenly a hope in your heart against hope that God will do what cannot be done by man. Write over your life, the wasted years of your life, "But we see Jesus." If your assembly has gone all a foul and you feel like you do not know whether they are alive or dead, write over that thing: "But we see Jesus, the Man in the glory that we are hooked to. He is the One who has begun a good work in us and He will complete it."

If we have seen this heavenly vision, if we have seen the Man in the glory, then suddenly we can look away onto Jesus. In Hebrews 12 it says we need to run the race, looking to Jesus. Most translations say, and actually more accurately, "Looking away," because we have to look away from some things we used to be quite taken with. But when we have seen the Man in glory, we can look away unto Jesus, the Author and Finisher of our faith. Once we have seen the Man in glory, we can press on to maturity. And the wonderful part that really opens the way in the whole letter to the Hebrews is that once we see the Man in glory, then suddenly He can come to us with very present help as we press on to maturity. Oh brethren, holy brethren, partakers of the heavenly calling, consider Jesus, the Apostle and High Priest of our confession.

THE HUMANITY OF JESUS

Now there is one thing we need to note and it is something quite unique to the book of Hebrews. This exhorter who has written this book under the inspiration of God has seen that which we need when we are pressing on to maturity is not only a sure vision of the Christ in glory who is divine, the Son of God seated at the right hand of the Majesty, but in a very practical way, if we are to press on to maturity, we have got to know the very human side of Christ the Son of Man, of Jesus the Son of Man.

There is a unique part of the book of Hebrews which I am sure you must have noticed but I will state it just in case you have never seen it this way before. It is interesting that within the New Testament, after the resurrection of Jesus, the name Christ Jesus, Lord Jesus, Lord Jesus Christ, Jesus the Son of God and other such divine appellations of Jesus are used more than seven hundred times throughout the rest of the New Testament. In other words, beyond the gospels you almost always find Jesus' name attached with His divinity or His Messianic office, Christ Jesus, Jesus Christ, Lord Jesus. From the gospels through to Revelation, Jesus is mentioned alone without another description twenty times, and ten of them are in Hebrews. When the word *Jesus* is used by itself, the writer is trying to focus on the humanity of Jesus. As surely as He is Christ and divine, He is our Lord and the Son of God, He is also human. And when you see the Man in the glory, it releases something in you like this: He is a human; I am a human. There is a possibility here. And then He comes to our aid as this very human Son of Man, dressed in these two offices, if you want to say, the office of the human high priest and the office of the human apostle to encourage us along the way. I will show you eight of the verses that are pretty clear just for our consideration so you can see these references to Jesus. Notice that every time you hear just the name of Jesus alone without some other reference or adjective you know this is referring to the human. He wants you to see the humanity of our precious Lord. You can never divorce one from the other, but we want to see His human side.

"But we see Jesus…" (Hebrews 2:9a). That is what it says in the Greek. "But we see Jesus crowned with glory and honor, made a little lower than the angels, by the grace of God tasting death for every man." Do you see Jesus?

"Consider Jesus, the Apostle and High Priest of our confession" (3:1b).

"Where Jesus has entered as a forerunner for us, having become a high priest forever according to the order of Melchizedek" (6:20).

"So much the more also Jesus has become the guarantee of a better covenant" (7:22).

"Therefore, brethren, since we have confidence to enter the holy place by the blood of Jesus" (10:19).

"Fixing our eyes on Jesus" (12:2a).

"And to Jesus, the mediator of a new covenant, and to the sprinkled blood, which speaks better than the blood of Abel" (12:24).

"Therefore Jesus also, that He might sanctify the people through His own blood, suffered outside the gate" (13:12).

What a wonderful vision this is! We must come to the place where we see that Jesus is a Man because it is only in that way that He can help us in pressing through. This is a very human divine transaction, this transformation, and the Man in glory has made it through. Now we can gain His aid. His finished work is involved in His divinity and His humanity, but His very present help was revealed to these dear saints who were in fear and trepidation: "Don't be afraid of Jesus; He does not bite. He is a human just like you."

JESUS—THE HIGH PRIEST

So when we consider Jesus the High Priest of this heavenly calling, we just want to notice three things. There is much to say from chapter 3 through chapter 10 concerning Jesus, the High Priest of our confession, but let's just look at three matters where Jesus the High Priest comes to us with help.

A Merciful High Priest

The first one that he shares is in chapter 2:14-18: "Since then the children share in flesh and blood, He Himself likewise also partook of the same, so that through death He might render powerless him who had the power of death, that is, the devil, and might free those who through fear of death were subject to slavery all their lives. For assuredly He does not give help to angels, but He gives help to the descendant of Abraham. Therefore, He had to be made like His brethren in all things, so that He might become a merciful and faithful high priest in things pertaining to God, to make propitiation for the sins of the people. For since He Himself was tempted in that which He has suffered, He is able to come to the aid of those who are tempted."

The first thing that the writer tries to underscore for us is that Jesus had to take on flesh and blood just like us with all the infirmity implicit in flesh and blood, which does not mean sinful flesh but humanness, in order that He might learn through the process of suffering in this life, how to be a merciful high priest. When we read chapter 5, we see the definition in spirit of what a high priest was supposed to be. The high priest in its purpose was a man of great gentleness, and he could understand the frailties of all those people who came around the tabernacle because he was beset by the same frailty. He could understand these people and pray for them. This is the nature of a high priest.

But the fact of the matter is that in Judaism the high priest had become haughty and proud; it was a position to fear. And to think of Jesus being the high priest for these Jews in this present day may have caused them to shrink back saying, "Oh my goodness, not another one of those guys, wearing the vestments, walking, strutting and proudly pushing people out of the way, commanding all reverence and being austere." But he says, "No, Jesus in His high priesthood took on flesh and blood so He could understand you and me, so He could become as he says here, a merciful and faithful high priest (v. 17). That is what people need.

And the first thing he is trying to show us is that it is as if He were standing as a priest inside the tabernacle. He hears some rustling out beyond the gate, and there are people out there who are fearful of coming in. They are fearful; their conscience is condemning them; they sense their temptation and how weak they are, and how they have fallen. They are afraid to come and even give an offering. They are afraid to come through the linen gate and come before the brazen altar. But you know what, this high priest has suffered and lived and been tempted just like those men outside. And so this wonderful high priest, being merciful and faithful, goes out and gathers them and convinces them to come on in: "It is okay. I understand. I can help you." And it seems that we find Christians in every quarter who are truly saved but they are on the outside of the tent looking in, and they feel so guilty about their sins. They hang back and live in the shadows beyond the curtains, and they are struggling with temptations. So Jesus said, "I have been there; I suffered; I was tempted in all ways like you, but I did not sin. But I understand.

Don't you think Jesus was tempted to hate? Don't you think Jesus was tempted to seek revenge? Don't you think Jesus was tempted to seek some way of saving Himself? Don't you think He was tempted by pride? Don't you think He was tempted by fear? He knows all these things that we suffer from, and yet He did not sin. But that does not mean He cannot deal gently with all those who are suffering such temptations and even in bondage to the enemy. The enemy has them so afraid of death that they cannot even live. But Jesus says, "You come to Me and I will let you live. Come to Me; let Me show you the way in." And so you can almost see this wonderful high priest going out beyond the curtain and bringing them in one by one. "Come, come, come, it is okay. I am not going to bite. I know what it is like. I have been there."

And it says in v. 18: "Since He Himself was tempted in that which He has suffered, He is able to come to the aid of those who are tempted." One translator said, "Because He understands He runs to every cry." Is that you crying? Maybe it is the lonely cry, the silent soul, the person who is afraid, almost afraid to believe that it would be possible that you could come in. You know what you have done wrong. You know how you have hurt people. More than that, you know you have sinned against God. This is the first thing we see about Jesus.

Those who deserve judgment discover the priest of mercy. He calls people in who nobody would dare call in. He is a merciful and faithful high priest. "You have been saved by My precious blood. I am going to bring you to glory, but first you have got to come in." So our Lord is so faithful. To the weak and the lonely He is not ashamed to say, "You are My child." He is not afraid or ashamed to call you brother if you will

only come. Don't stay outside. Don't stay outside.
There is only the way forward.

The High Priest Brings Us In

Then we turn to chapter 4 and we find the
second wonderful picture of this high priest
again. It is quite similar yet there is something
wonderfully different here.

"Since then we have a great high priest who
has passed through the heavens, Jesus the Son of
God, let us hold fast our confession. For we do
not have a high priest who cannot sympathize
with our weaknesses, but One who has been
tempted in all things as we are, yet without sin.
Therefore let us draw near with confidence to
the throne of grace, so that we may receive
mercy and find grace to help in time of need"
(Hebrews 4:14-16).

This is the high priest job if I could put it in
just one word. The high priest is the one who
enables us and helps us to *draw nigh*. Those two
words we see in v. 16: "Therefore let us draw
near..." This is the job of this wonderful high
priest.

Look at it again in 7:19: "(For the Law made nothing perfect), and on the other hand there is a bringing in of a better hope, through which we draw near to God."

Our desire is to draw near to God, but it is Jesus the faithful high priest that enables us to get there.

Hebrews 7:25a: "Therefore He is able also to save forever those who draw near to God."

10:1: "For the Law, since it has only a shadow of the good things to come and not the very form of things, can never, by the same sacrifices which they offer continually year by year, make perfect those who draw near." No amount of sacrifices can do that but His one sacrifice can.

10:21-22a: "Since we have a great priest over the house of God, let us draw near."

The high priest's job is to bring us in. What is He preparing us for? In our road to glory in this heavenly calling, in the first half of it, and a very essential half of it is this: God wants us drawing nigh unto Him, drawing right into the holy of holies. That is where we belong; that is where we must go. The mature would press on with the help of their high priest all the way into the holiest where we abide. How precious is this high priest!

It says in 4:15, "We do not have a high priest who cannot sympathize." It is interesting that the Greek word is exactly that, *sumpatheo* which means "who cannot suffer with us." We do not have a high priest who cannot suffer with us, but one who understands us, was tempted in all ways like we are, yet without sin. And so here is what this precious high priest does. He brings us to the throne. We would not dare come by ourselves, but He brings us to the throne of grace, especially those in time of need.

Did you notice that in v. 16: "Let us draw near with confidence to the throne of grace, so that we may receive mercy and find grace to help in time of need." So often we stay away as long as we can but when the need gets great enough, we can find our way, stumble in somehow to that throne of grace. That should not be the way it is. This throne of grace is not just for those with an occasional need; this throne of grace is for the pilgrim who is pressing on to maturity with a need every day, for the further you go the more you sense your weakness.

Get into the throne, get into the throne! And so this high priest brings us daily into the throne until we can come into that throne with boldness and receive the grace and the mercy that we need for that day. Don't think it is a provision for those in need or some special provision on special occasion. This should be our daily portion before the throne of grace, taking what we need to press on to maturity. Have you done that? Do you have the boldness to go every day to the throne? "Lord, I need Your grace today. Lord, I need Your grace today more than I did yesterday. There is more upon me, and I cannot live except by Your life. And oh Lord, have mercy." This is our provision and the high priest brings us in where we would not dare to go.

Along the same line, He is the high priest who is ever making intercession for us. He is praying for us when we have no knowledge of it, and this whole thing is that He is trying to draw us near unto God. He is the mediator of the new covenant, and that mediator simply means He closes the gap. If there is any gap between you and God He closes that gap. He takes God's word and brings it from your mind down into your heart so that you come to know Him as we all know Him in that better covenant. He is the mediator. He brings us through. He shows us the way. He walks us through this thing. How do you know how to live in the new covenant? You need somebody to walk you through.

I live in Manhattan now, less than a quarter mile from New York University. This girl came to register at NYU as a freshman, and it is a daunting task. If you go over there on your own, you end up going to the wrong building and the class is closed out by the time you get to the right building. Then the bursar is closed by the time you try to make a payment. Some people go there for two days; they get lost in the place and can't even find their way out, and nothing happens by the time it is over. But this dear girl came and she stayed with my wife and me. She was going over there to register the next day, shaking in her boots, but one of the saints who had been to NYU said, "Let me walk you through it." Two hours later she came back and had all the classes she needed, paid all the debt she owed, walked through just as easy as could be, because somebody walked her through.

The high priest walks us through. We do not know how to go in this way. Don't think the high priest is sitting upon a throne saying, "Come on up here. Come on. You can make it. Chin up! Up, up, up." No, no, that is not it at all. He is the great encourager of our souls. He is the one who comes alongside us and says, "Let Me help you along the way." Are you willing to take this humble help? Or are we too proud? "No, no, I can take it from here, Jesus. Please don't bother." You will find yourself in trouble by the time you turn the corner. Oh, how we need this high priest. He is so available to us if we would only take it and begin to live in the good of the new covenant. How wonderful! We read these words of the new covenant, and they are so wonderful, they are almost unbelievable. There is no more transgression. God is known by us. It is so wonderful, but please, can somebody walk me through this?

The High Priest Brings Us to the Living God

And then if that is not enough, the last one I would like to share is the wonderful passage in chapter 10:19-22a: "Therefore, brethren, since we have confidence to enter the holy place by the blood of Jesus, by a new and living way which He inaugurated for us through the veil, that is, His flesh, and since we have a great priest over the house of God, let us draw near."

Oh, wonderful thought! And here is a saint, a dear worshiper, who is bid to draw nigh, but it is into the holiest place with the living God. Now who dares go in? The priest in the Old Testament economy did not dare go in, and the high priest went into because he had to once a year. But it was a fearful thing to go before the living God. We are not talking about the holiest place where Jesus is. Of course that is where He dwells, but we are talking about the holiest place where the Father dwells. How are we going to get to the Father and worship the Father in spirit and in truth unless we have a high priest who walks us through from the outer court, helps us wash our hands, get into the holy place, offer the right sacrifice, and even though the veil is open, we

106

dare not go in unless Jesus says, "No, I am right by your side, carrying My precious blood. Let's go right into the holiest place." And there you are right before the living God. Now that will bring maturity through transformation into your life as fast as anything ever would, and it is our privilege as worshipers to take that route boldly by this new and living way through the precious blood and the rent veil. But I do not see Christians going in there unless they are arm in arm with this High Priest. This is the picture again in the Old Testament of the child of God needing the encouragement of the priest to get in there to the house of God. You cannot make it alone. You do not know the way; there are too many places you are supposed to bow and curtsey.

About two months ago my son who lives in London, England had a meeting with the Queen, very posh thing. They went to this dinner and stood in a line and met the Queen and Prince Phillip, and Prince Phillip laughed at something my son said, and they ended up talking about five or ten minutes. Then later on in the evening the Queen and the Prince came by again. Before he went they gave my son two pages of instructions. You do not talk unless she talks to you. You curtsey, you bow. You do not say "ma'am," you do not say this; this you say. There is such a rigmarole, you would not believe it.

And there is divine order in the house of God, and even if we would press in to that holy of holies, there is a way through. We dare not go by ourselves. We do not know the way so well. Our Lord Jesus says, "Come on; I know My Father. Let me show you My Father." And we go in, and we find that the Father's throne is the throne of grace after all. Jesus is sitting at the right hand, and the Father is as gracious as the Son. This is incredible to believe. But as our High Priest Jesus is so human. He wants to help us so much. Whose heart will be humble and ask for that help? We want to go on and press on to maturity, but that sounds like big and heavy words. But our dear High Priest is waiting for us to take us by the hand. Oh, may we hear the heavenly calling. It all begins when we see the Man in glory, and we see ourselves in the glory. You are only right to ever go in there because Jesus purchased your way in. So go with Him. He wants to lead us in.

Who ever heard of such a gospel? It is so good. Who can believe it? Here is a God who came down from heaven and died for our sins because we were just going to hell. He died for our sins and rose again, and He is sitting in the glory. That is the same guy, Jesus. Not only that but He comes down to us because we sort of wander outside the tent, sort of fearful to get started.

Many teenagers have so many temptations, so many hormones pushing them this way and that, so many distractions and potentials and everything. How can they set their course? It is almost impossible. They just hang around outside, peeking through the window, and Jesus, that high priest, goes outside to get them. Don't think you can get outside His curtains. If you are saved, He knows who you are. He will bring you in because He is a merciful High Priest. Then He will bring you to the throne of grace until you get used to it. Then you can come boldly and always come with Him and find grace and mercy.

Then of course when you come to worship, He says, "Let Me lead you in there to worship. Otherwise, you get scared away by some of those angels fluttering around. Some of the things going on is a different kind of atmosphere. You just stick with Me." Sometimes our kids are afraid to do something. Occasionally there is a chasm to walk over or something. The parents can do it but the kid is afraid. But when you have the kid right here, then the kid is not afraid. Oh, it is not time for us to be afraid, but it is time to consider Jesus, the High Priest of our confession, a time to see the Man in glory, to see ourselves in glory according to the Father's pleasure and purpose.

Oh dear brothers and sisters, if you have not seen the glory, there is a Spirit who wants to reveal Jesus to you in all His glory if you will just come and ask. Have you seen Him, heard Him, known Him? Is not thine a captive heart? For this we pray in Jesus' name. Amen.

JESUS AS THE APOSTLE

Lord, as we come to You, we thank You for so great a salvation that we have in Jesus Christ even presented before us as we sat around His table. Thank You for all that You have given us so freely by Your sacrifice. And You have even given us an anointing for this meeting, refreshment for our bodies, illumination for our minds, and a heart to obey. Oh Lord, we take all these things and more; all Your provisions are the best; in Jesus' precious name. Amen.

Hebrews   3:1-4:1-13—Therefore,   holy brethren, partakers of a heavenly calling, consider Jesus, the Apostle and High Priest of our confession. He was faithful to Him who appointed Him, as Moses also was in all His house. For He has been counted worthy of more glory than Moses, by just so much as the builder of the house has more honor than the house. For every house is built by someone, but the builder of all things is God. Now Moses was faithful in all His house as a servant, for a testimony of those things which were to be spoken later; but Christ was faithful as a Son over His house—whose house we are, if we hold fast our confidence and the boast of our hope firm until the end. Therefore, just as the Holy Spirit says,

"Today if you hear His voice, do not harden your hearts as when they provoked Me, as in the day of trial in the wilderness, where your fathers tried Me by testing Me, and saw My works for forty years. Therefore I was angry with this generation, and said, 'they always go astray in their heart, and they did not know My ways;' as I swore in My wrath, 'they shall not enter My rest."

Take care, brethren, that there not be in any one of you an evil, unbelieving heart that falls away from the living God. But encourage one another day after day, as long as it is still called 'Today,' so that none of you will be hardened by the deceitfulness of sin. For we have become partakers of Christ, if we hold fast the beginning of our assurance firm until the end, while it is said,

"Today if you hear His voice, do not harden your hearts, as when they provoked Me."

For who provoked Him when they had heard? Indeed, did not all those who came out of Egypt led by Moses? And with whom was He angry for forty years? Was it not with those who sinned, whose bodies fell in the wilderness? And to whom did He swear that they would not enter His rest, but to those who were disobedient? So we see that they were not able to enter because of unbelief. Therefore, let us fear if, while a promise remains of entering His rest, any one of you may seem to have come short of it. For indeed we have had good news preached to us, just as they also; but the word they heard did not profit them, because it was not united by faith in those who heard. For we who have believed enter that rest, just as He has said,

"As I swore in My wrath, they shall not enter My rest,"

although His works were finished from the foundation of the world. For He has said somewhere concerning the seventh day:

"And God rested on the seventh day from all His works;"

And again in this passage,

"They shall not enter My rest."

Therefore, since it remains for some to enter it, and those who formerly had good news preached to them failed to enter because of disobedience, He again fixes a certain day,

"Today," saying through David after so long a time just as has been said before,

"Today if you hear His voice, do not harden your hearts."

For if Joshua had given them rest, He would not have spoken of another day after that. So there remains a Sabbath rest for the people of God. For the one who has entered His rest has himself also rested from his works, as God did from His. Therefore let us be diligent to enter that rest, so that no one will fall, through following the same example of disobedience. For the word of God is living and active and sharper than any two-edged sword, and piercing as far as the division of soul and spirit, of both joints and marrow, and able to judge the thoughts and intentions of the heart. And there is no creature hidden from His sight, but all things are open and laid bare to the eyes of Him with whom we have to do.

Hebrews 12:1-7—Therefore, since we have so great a cloud of witnesses surrounding us, let us also lay aside every [weight] and the sin which so easily entangles us, and let us run with [patience] the race that is set before us, fixing our eyes on Jesus, the author and perfecter of faith, who for the joy set before Him endured the cross, despising the shame, and has sat down at the right hand of the throne of God. For consider Him who has endured such hostility by sinners against Himself, so that you will not grow weary and lose heart. You have not yet resisted to the point of shedding blood in your striving against sin, and you have forgotten the exhortation which is addressed to you as sons,

"My son, do not regard lightly the discipline of the Lord, nor faint when you are reproved by Him; for those whom the Lord loves He disciplines, and He scourges every son whom He receives."

It is for discipline that you endure; God deals with you as with sons; for what son is there whom his father does not discipline?

115

Hebrews 13:10-14—We have an altar from which those who serve the tabernacle have no right to eat. For the bodies of those animals whose blood is brought into the holy place by the high priest as an offering for sin, are burned outside the camp. Therefore Jesus also, that He might sanctify the people through His own blood, suffered outside the gate. So let us go out to Him outside the camp, bearing His reproach. For here we do not have a lasting city, but we are seeking the city which is to come.

We have read just a few of the strong exhortations that we find in the letter to the Hebrews. Exhortations are very strong, but the shaking that is to come will prove if we have heard and heeded the exhortations. In chapter 6:1 we are told to press on to maturity, and this pressing on is a very deliberate act. Basically, this great salvation that we have presented to us in this letter, this pressing on to maturity, reduces itself down to one thing. Our full confidence that is in Jesus Christ our Lord has not only the all-sufficient sacrifice for our sins but the all-sufficient Savior who can save us to the uttermost. So we press on into maturity.

The way we begin to move towards maturity is really not by some self-initiative but rather by a response to something we see that draws us forward. Many of us begin the Christian life by knowing the Lord Jesus as our Savior, by knowing His salvation, and we start to walk with the Lord Jesus. But somewhere along the way, maybe during a message or a communion, during a prayer at home, or perhaps while reading a book, something opens. The heavens open, and we suddenly realize that we have grossly underestimated the greatness of our salvation, the greatness of our Savior, the greatness of the eternal purpose, and the greatness of our calling. Something opens to us. As the writer of Hebrews puts it: "But we see Jesus."

After seeing the failure of man to be perfected according to the purpose God had for him, we see Jesus, the first Man in glory, the first One to make it through, the first Man as man in flesh and blood to live on this earth without sin. And having passed the test of all the temptations that mankind is shown, He went to the cross and died for our sins according to God's wonderful plan to bring many sons to glory. Now, after having risen and been victorious, He sits at the right hand of the Father. What a wonderful picture of the Man in the glory and of the worship that we bear!

This vision is necessary in our lives as a sort of motivational way of getting us forward. And we find as we begin to pursue the Lord that He meets us along the way in increasing amounts as we are able to bear it. This vision of glory that we see so wonderfully in the lives of people like the apostle Paul or Isaiah or Stephen or others, these quintessential visions and openings of heaven and the glory of Christ they saw is not the experience of most of us. But it is not some experience that is only the exclusive domain of a few mystics.

The Holy Spirit's primary job right now is to bring us into all the truth of Christ, to take the things of Christ and present them to us, or as Paul would put it, "There is a spirit of wisdom and revelation in the knowledge of Jesus Christ that is revealing Christ in His glory to us." It is not just the Savior as He walked upon the earth, meek and mild, the gospel-Jesus that we know, but it is the Jesus above, the Jesus whom John the beloved disciple saw and fell down as dead. But when we see the Christ of glory, there is a change in our lives and an upgrade in our calling and a different attitude toward the things of God according to His purpose. This bringing many sons to glory sounds like some kind of pie in the sky thing, but you see that this is really the Lord's plan and He locks hold of your life and begins to work in that very direction.

When I started off as a Christian, I felt called to the ministry. I went into seminary and came out on the other side as a Baptist minister. I loved the Lord and I preached the gospel, but I had no idea the church was the glorious church. I just thought the church was a good Baptist church, the best church around. The way we do things is all right. We have people come up and they either give us a letter from another Baptist church or we dunk them in the water. We had a good thing going. But it was a kind of rough and tumble church, with a whole lot of fighting going on and the deacons working out some things. Every year we would have to conscript Sunday

School teachers, which was not very spiritual, but you had to do it. So you found a woman who could read and write and she was the third grade teacher; that was it. That is the way we looked at it, a kind of rugged thing, but we loved the saints.

Then to my surprise, one day, by the mercy of God, as I saw the Lord Jesus in a much higher way, I also saw His church. I saw that He was really serious about a glorious church, and suddenly my standards changed. I was not satisfied with what I saw, so being a pastor I tried to change it twelve different ways, and it only made it worse. Then, of course, I saw that the primary problem with this configuration was me, and so began a whole kind of re-understanding of what it means to be called in this heavenly calling. You have to see it or else you are quite satisfied with the way things are. If you have a good kind of ministry and you are serving God in some way, you are all very happy about it, until you see the Lord's desire. It is not like the Lord's standards, it is not His legalistic level of acceptability; it is what His heart wants. And when we see what His heart wants, then we have to decide what to do about it.

From that time on I found it very hard, in fact, it was impossible for me to stay in a denominational configuration because it was not responding to the Lord Jesus' heart. Since that day I have never seen a perfect congregation, but I have seen some people, scraggly as they may be, who really want to satisfy the Lord Jesus' heart so much so that I believe if the Lord said, "Now I see this wrong," as He said to Ephesus or Thyatira, they would repent and ask the Lord to deal with them. Now that is the best we can hope for at this time. The Lord has a process going on, but the point is unless you see the glorious church you have no motivation to do anything other than what you already have. And that is all part of this Man in the glory that we have been talking about.

THE HIGH PRIEST

We spoke about seeing the glorious High Priest. Of course the High Priest ministered to us just now. The High Priest's call to us morning, noon, and night by the Spirit of God on our bed and when we first awake is: "Draw nigh unto Me." When we go to bed or when we wake in the morning, there is that still small voice of our precious High Priest saying, "Draw nigh." And we simply saw this picture as Hebrews uniquely reveals the very human side of Jesus and His struggling to learn obedience and His sufferings He went through as a human being. The whole point being that Jesus says, "Come to Me."

You say, "No, no, no, I am too sinful."

"Come to Me."

"No, no, I already came to You and I left You. No, no, no."

"Come to Me."

And if you see the Man in the glory, you see that the eyes of this High Priest are filled with tender mercy, and you come. Then He says, "Now draw near to the throne of grace. You need grace; you need mercy. Come, come with Me; I will show you where it is." And He takes you into the throne of grace, and you find yourself before God who is full of grace and He offers it to you. Then having done that He says, "There is one more place we should really go."

You say, "What is that?"

He says, "Let's go to the holy of holies."

"No, no, no, I am not dressed properly."

He says, "You are coming by My blood. Let Me take you by the hand and lead you in to the holy of holies before an unseen God, and you can worship Him." Only such a glorified Man, such a Man of understanding and patience and love could bring us in. But we always hear His voice, "Draw nigh, draw nigh." And so we could say, "A real mark of maturity is how often we draw near. It is that crucial to our lives. Of course, everybody here has a work-a-day life. You have to go to work; you have to raise the kids. You have got to do whatever you have to do. That is fine; but have you drawn nigh? It is a mark of maturity because after a while you learn it has nothing to do with my worthiness or unworthiness. It has nothing to do with my preparedness or my un-preparedness. The precious blood has opened the way and by grace I just need to come and grab the hand of my High Priest and say, "Take me into the Father, please." It is a very humbling thing to be a Christian for forty-three years and still say, "Jesus, would You take me into the Father, please." We shall be doing that today and forever.

The enemy contests this drawing nigh, and one of the ways he would try to rob us is to keep you away from that throne of grace so that you have a nice ungracious faith, to keep you from worshiping in the holy of holies, to keep you outside banging a tambourine in the outer court. There are all kinds of things in your own mind and there are all kinds of things that are dead set against you drawing nigh. There is the Law that tells you who you are, and grace that tells you who He is. Now, who are you going to listen to? Your conscience says, "Look inside of you, you dirty, rotten person." You start to mess around with your conscience very long and the next thing you know there is a lot of lint in the belly button and there is no way that you can draw near. But the Spirit says, "Look away to the blood of Jesus." You have to make your choice. We have got to move ourselves beyond our introspection and our lousy feelings. It is not a question of being unworthy. Of course, we are unworthy. It is a question of what He has provided for us as the High Priest.

THE APOSTLE OF OUR CONFESSION

Now we want to consider this glorious Son of Man as Jesus the Apostle of our confession. This Man in the glory is also the Apostle of our salvation. We have seen the Apostle while He was on earth treading the way of the cross and opening the way before us. The Apostle treads the way and opens the way for us to come to salvation. We saw that in the Apostle when He was here upon the earth, but now we need to see the Apostle in His glory in heaven because now that you are saved and you have seen the Apostle of the gospels, He wants you to see the glorious Apostle who would bring us to perfection. And if the watch word of the High Priest was, "Draw nigh unto Me," the watchword of the Apostle is, "Look unto Jesus, the Author and Finisher of your faith." No matter what, look unto Jesus; look away unto Jesus, the Author and Finisher of your faith.

The same grace that would bid us come into the holiest also leads us outside the camp. We are to live in the holiest and outside the camp. Most Christians live outside the holiest and inside the camp. But according to Hebrews 13 you do not find Jesus in the camp. He had to go outside the camp and the exhortation is, "Won't you meet Him out there?"

Jesus is outside the camp. Now the camp in this book of Hebrews was, of course, first and foremost Judaism which rejected Jesus and threw Him out. But it is strange how Christendom has a dislike of the Lord Jesus, and surely in these last days, as we are in the phase of the Laodicean age, our Lord Jesus is outside knocking on the door where people are not listening because they are self-satisfied. But this Apostle wants to bring us unto maturity. We are partakers of the heavenly calling, and we are always to be looking away to Jesus. And the issue is the perfecting of our faith, looking unto Jesus the Author and Perfecter of our faith. You were saved by grace and that was His authorship by His finished work. But He wants your faith perfected, and He is the Apostle who is well able to do it.

We are going to look at the Apostle whose job is already finished but just like as the High Priest who saves us to the uttermost, now as the Apostle He brings many sons to glory. That is His job. Enthroned in glory this Man as an Apostle will bring many sons to glory by His ministrations. We will only look at two as illustrations.

The first one is that He perfects our faith by leading us into His rest, and the second is that He perfects our faith as we run the race unto sonship.

THE APOSTLE LEADS US INTO HIS REST

The first one is in the Scriptures we read in chapter 3 and 4. You are aware that this is the story from the Old Testament. We have the story of Israel's sojourn coming out of Egypt, going through the wilderness, and going into the promised land. And this is the illustration that the author is using to try to show us where we need to get to—Canaan Land, the rest, the glory land. That is the picture before us here, and Moses is the apostle. Indeed, he is the apostle; indeed he is a faithful apostle; indeed he is an apostle who has been arrested himself by a vision of glory, not only there in a burning bush but then again upon a mountain. Moses had such fellowship with this wonderful Jehovah who called Himself "Jehovah, Jehovah God, compassionate and merciful, slow to anger, and abounding in mercy," that he said, "Show me Thy glory." The Lord said, "I am sorry; I can only show you the back. If you saw the whole thing you would be frizzed." But Moses saw something of His glory. He was caught. From then on he was caught. It did not matter how troublesome the children were because he saw God's children and God's plan too. God was trying to gather them together and draw them to Himself and make His children His possession, make them a kingdom of priests. Moses saw that purpose. And while he was on the mountain in this momentary glory, he not only saw the Lord but he also saw His purpose and His house. So Moses saw the house, and he had to build according to the pattern of what he saw. That is all part of that glorious purpose that he saw upon the mount, and he was faithful, no doubt about it.

But Moses could not bring the children into Canaan's rest. He could not do it, but you could hardly say it was his fault. The children as God's possession had everything going for them. They had the presence of God, the fire by night and the cloud by day. They had the promise of God: "Go in and take the land flowing with milk and honey. This is your rest; this is your inheritance; go get it, I am with you." They had the promise of the word, they had the presence of God, and they had the daily provision as they walked through the wilderness. They even had the order all worked out, who was to go in first, what tribe was to go ahead, and the war. They had all of that—the promises, the presence, the word, and the apostle, but they got to Kadesh-barnea, and they could not go in. They did not accept the minority reports of Joshua and Caleb, and they could not go in. They could not mix it with faith as it says in Hebrews 4:2: "Indeed we had good news preached to us just as they also but the word they heard did not profit them because it was not mixed with faith in those who heard." So the Lord said, "You shall not enter My rest."

As you follow this story through chapter 4 you see that even when Joshua finally brought them into the promised land he brought them into the outside. Indeed it was Canaan but he still did not bring them into rest. How could they rest? They had no king and everybody was doing what was right in their own eyes. So they were in Canaan but they were not enjoying it. That is why David said centuries later, "God is still waiting for us to enter His rest." That is sort of the point of the Old Testament story here.

"But now we have Jesus, the Apostle." Now He is not just a servant in the house of God; He owns the house of God, whose house we are, and He is a better Apostle in every way. His design is to bring many sons to glory and bring the Christians into Canaan's rest.

THE MILLENNIUM REST

What is Canaan's rest? It is at least two things we know because this is talking about growth or maturity. The rest that he is talking about finally is the millennium rest, the kingdom rest, coming into our inheritance in the kingdom through abiding faithfulness in Christ. The reward of faithfully walking with the Apostle is that you enjoy the inheritance in the kingdom when our Lord comes back. I do not know if you think that is going to happen but I do, so that makes me happy. There is going to be Jesus returning and setting up His kingdom, and there is a place in the inheritance for those who have been faithful.

THE PERFECTING OF THE SAINTS

But as many Scriptures as there are to that ultimate fulfillment, there is the immediate fulfillment for the Christian of entering into His rest even while on this earth. There is an enjoying of the land of Christ as your inheritance, even though imperfectly as you tread the hills and vales of all that Christ is, and this is to be our portion too. And I always feel like when I am here I am preaching to the choir because so many of you have tasted the milk and the honey. You know just a little something about the land of Canaan, the land of Christ in His goodness and fullness. Some live in the good of it even and rejoice that they have found their rest. But many, many Christians have no idea there is a Canaan Land in this lifetime. They are saved and just holding on by the skin of their teeth until they die and can go to heaven because they have no prospect of any maturity really in their lives except to pray and keep giving and a couple of things like that.

Here we find the picture of these Christians. What do we have? We have the better Apostle. We have the Man in the glory, the Apostle Jesus, the One who is going to lead us into the Canaan Land. What else do we have? We also have the promises; we also have the presence of God; we also have the apostles. And yet the warning is that it is possible to be the church, the house of God and be out of Egypt but not be in the promised land, to be stuck in the middle somewhere, halfway out and halfway in. This is a problem of our faith needing to be perfected. Isn't it strange as the Lord is dealing with us to be perfected, that this is the way He decides to perfect you?

"Okay," He says, "here you go, Joe; I am going to perfect you and here is the way I am going to do it. I am going to throw you in with a whole mob. It is My household. We have new ones and old ones. We have spiritual ones and carnal ones. We have zealous ones and lukewarm ones. And that is where I am putting you to be perfected." I cannot imagine anything being more impatient than being Caleb and Joshua with this sorry bunch. They could have gone in thirty-eight years before the rest of them. They were ready at Kadesh-barnea, two years out of Egypt, and they had to wait another thirty-eight years for all the rest of them to catch up. And that is exactly the situation that perfected Joshua and made him able to bring them in in the end, thirty-eight wasted years for God's preparation. There is a lot of mystery in all of this. I am not saying that the Scriptures are altogether clear about this mystery of bringing many sons to glory, but it is when we find these little clues we can find help in this.

And so the children of God, the Christians today can get stuck in that halfway place. They are out but they are not in, and the question is: what more do we need? "Ah, yes, we need more faith."

Well, okay.

"How about our need for more of the word of God? That is what we need. That is what is going to do it."

"We need more promises. I only have a thousand promises in my promise box; get me another two hundred and we can make it in."

Is that what we need?

"How about more of God's presence?"

Ah yes, the presence of God is something everybody is talking about now in the worship time.

"How about more time? Oh yes, it would work out if we just had a little more time."

"How about more obedience?"

"Or how about just having some other leader?"

That became the children of Israel's complaint: "We have the wrong leader and that is why we are going nowhere. Can we do better than this apostle we have?"

THE FLESH HAS TO DIE

The Lord Jesus is our Apostle; why can't we go in? This is the lesson that we have to learn in our maturing process. In fact we cannot go in, and you know what the reason is, don't you? Our Apostle wants to take us in but we have misnamed the Apostle because we call Him Jesus the Apostle and Perfecter of our faith. But in this case we have to realize how He takes us into Canaan Land, and it is this. It is Jesus Christ and Him crucified that brings us into the promise. It is Christ crucified, and until we understand that, we cannot go in. Of course, you know flesh cannot inherit the kingdom of God, and what we have in this wilderness of church life is a lot of flesh, a lot of arguing, a lot of murmuring, a lot of ideas, and just like with the children of Israel, that has all got to die. It cannot go into the promised land. But we all think that our ideas are the right ideas. I am going to fight you about it until I die. And the Lord says in Hebrews 12:1-2, which is the model as it were for following the Apostle: "Let us run the race set before us, fixing our eyes on Jesus, the author and perfecter of faith, who for the joy set before Him endured the cross, suffering the shame, and has sat down at the right hand of the throne of God."

That is how the Apostle made it through into glory. How are we going to make it through into glory? We have to be crucified; our flesh has got to die or we are not going in. This is the lesson of maturity that we learn. We have this idea that the Lord would say to us as the Apostle: "I would never send you anywhere that I have not already trod, but now that I have trod I whistle back to you, 'Come, I have already opened the way, come on let's go.'" But somehow we cannot make it through because we always have this idea of a separated God from us who is calling us up hither as it were. But if you can understand the way I am trying to put it, He would never say, "I would never send you some place where I have not gone." He would never send you. Why would He send you? "I would never send you but I will take you with Me into the promised land." Now that is a whole other thing, and this is all part of this learning of how to live by the life of Christ. Something has got to be crucified, and something has got to live. Our flesh is not going to make it into this land of promise, into glory, into rest, but He said, "Oh no, I am not going to tell you to come in, but I will take you in if you let Me." And we begin to learn that we can obey in His life, and He will bring us in.

THE LIVING WORD

This leads us to the secondary point in the same issue of learning how to live by His life and not by our own. It is the same thing regarding the word of God. We think that we should hear the word and we say, "Okay, I am going to obey the word. I hear the word; I will obey the word." It is true in a very simple way that is what happens. But if we are talking about going into glory it is a little more complicated than that because the word that tells you, "Go into glory," is impossible for us. And whenever He gives a word that is impossible, there is only one thing to do. You have to say, "Lord, I cannot do it, but You can do it. I believe in Your word; I put my full trust in Your word." I do not know if you have experienced it but the reality is that the word begins to take you into the reality of it. We have this mentality today, and it is a very popular thing in the move of God today to talk about heroes. What we need is heroes, anointed men and women standing up by faith obeying the word of God and crashing through the barriers. It is a very noble thing and people get stirred up. Young people love this idea of having a hero because a lot of them think they can be that.

I will never forget the first time I heard this brother, Major Ian Thomas, and he was muttering in his English accent in such a way it was hard to hear him unless you really listened. But after a while my ear tuned in and he told the story about how he first came to understand he had to live but not him, he had to live by the life of Christ in him. He was already a servant of God, so it came down to the Lord saying, "I want you to go down there and witness to the students at the University of London."

And he said, "No Lord, I cannot go."

And the Lord said, "But I want you to go."

Then he said, "I am going to go because You want me to go, but I do not know what I am suppose to say."

The Lord said, "That is okay; I will tell you what to say."

And he started learning the exchanged life by a dialogue of recognizing his impossibility and then turning it over to the Lord and trusting His possibility. Do you understand that? Now if we are going to grow we need to grow past this idea that what we need is more faith in some kind of a noble hero. "Whatever You say, Lord. Aye, aye, sir." And He tells you to do impossible things. Wisdom realizes that what you say is, "Well Lord, You are telling me something that only You can do, so I am going to hang on to Your life. And if this is Your word, then I believe it and I trust Your word. Now You take me into it."

When you look at the lives of the men, the champions of faith, heroes of faith in Hebrews 11, you find some people who just submitted to what God told them: "I say you are going to have a kid." "Well okay." After trying this way and that, Abraham said, "I guess it is time for me to believe God. I have gone this way and that way and that did not work." He did not immediately start a kind of honeymoon campaign to have a kid. No, God told him. Abraham just said, "God, I trust Your word and I will live my life normally, and by Your word You bring me into that," because His word is living.

At the end of this whole story about entering into His rest, we find out that he says, "And so we cease from our works and enter His rest, and the word of God is living and active and sharper than any two-edged sword." If we let the living word do its work in us, it will bring us to obedience. I do not say that you just hear the word and go away and be a forgetful hearer. You hold on to the word and say, "Now Lord, that is Your word and I am holding onto it because only you can bring me into it." That is how we go through the Jordan—hold on to the word. If you hold onto the word it will give you enough oxygen when you are under the water to bring you through. And so we come into rest.

Our Apostle, this glorious Man in glory, is the crucified Christ, and you can see that everything you achieve in the way of abundance, in the way of rest, and in the way of the life of Canaan is achieved through death and resurrection. As a matter of fact, by the grace of God, when we end up on the other side in Canaan Land and we are experiencing a whole new kind of life, we have to discover how to live on resurrection ground because we are so used to living on the old decayed ground on the other side. That is why we can get into the promised land and yet not enjoy it because we do not have a rest in it.

What is this word of rest? Of course, it says in Hebrews 4:1: "Let us therefore fear, lest, a promise being left of entering into His rest." It is not our rest; it is His rest, but it becomes our rest if we are in His rest. He completed the work. If we rest in Him, His completed work makes us work the best. Somebody who has entered into that rest has ceased from his own works as God has from His. And when you cease from your own work, that is when your works are the most effective and the most frequent, because when it is His rest and it is His work, it is completely different. Only the Lord can bring us into this wonderful life, possessing Christ, wanting to know Him, studying His words, standing on His word, trusting in His word, finding the obedience to His word by His life within us. It is an amazing life. It is a glorious life. It is the best life, living in the better plains.

RUN THE RACE SET BEFORE YOU

Let's finish by looking at the passage in Hebrews 12 because here is the second picture we have. Here we find that our Apostle, the Man in the glory is running with us, but not two miles ahead, saying, "I have already had My run; go ahead, you run now." The Apostle is so patient; He runs two miles an hour if that is all you can do. Run with patience, run with endurance the race that is set before you.

What is the race that is set before you? It is the race of bringing you unto glory. That is the race that is set before you in the book of Hebrews. It is not the race of your ministry or the race of your marriage or the race of your schooling; it is the race of God's purpose in you to bring you to glory. And you have got to run that race with patience; you have got to run it with endurance, but you have to run it with Jesus the Apostle. He knows how to run you through this course because from the moment we are Christians we are now the sons of God, as it says in I John 3:2a "Now we are the sons of God and it has not appeared as yet what we will be. We know that when He appears, we will be like Him."

DISCIPLINE OF THE HOLY SPIRIT

It is true, we have been bought with the precious blood and we are the children and the sons of God, but this matter of becoming sons is a question of maturity. It is a matter that involves discipline, the discipline of the Holy Spirit. This throws off many Christians when they begin to be disciplined by the Lord whom they thought loved them. And they faint and say, "The Lord does not love me anymore." But here is the deal, we have been saved, it is true, and we are living as a new self. This new self has been formed and created in the image of God. We have a new self and a new life and a new being, but this new life needs to be disciplined. When we start out, our spirit is so weak. He wants to strengthen our inner man, but there is a discipline involved of the word, prayer, understanding, and exercise of obedience. All of this strengthens the inner man that is so weak.

It says in chapter 12:12: " Strengthen the hands that are weak." Now they are not bad hands, they are not evil hands; they are just the weak hands of somebody who needs the discipline and exercise of service. That is what the hands are all about.

"And strengthen the knees that are feeble." We begin as Christians, as children of God but our walk is a little bit feeble, a little bit wobbly. So what is the exhortation that comes from the Spirit of God? Strengthen the knees; don't just walk on your knees. "Wait, hang on I will get you a bicycle." No, this is the discipline of the Spirit, and He begins to strengthen the things that are weak through a process of discipline.

When we are running the race, we never get past the fact that we need to lay aside weights. After we have done a lap and come around we say, "I have got to get rid of this sweat suit." We take another lap around and say, "These knee high sneakers are too high, I have got to trim them down." So we are always going to have to get rid of weights, these weighty things that we have in our lives that are part of the trimming process; not to mention the besetting sins that creep in throughout our lives. It is never that we stop dealing with sin and things, but I am talking about a positive discipline of the new man that you are. It still needs to be disciplined. Our minds are renewed but they need to be illuminated. There is a process here, and the Spirit of God is faithful in disciplining our lives unto maturity. That is how we become sons.

The Spirit says, "Okay, strengthen those legs. Come on walk the straight walk." The Spirit of God is sent by the Apostle. How else are we going to share His holiness unless we are disciplined?

"They disciplined us for a short time as seemed best to them, but He disciplines us for our good, so that we may share His holiness. All discipline for the moment seems not to be joyful, but sorrowful; yet to those who have been trained by it, afterwards it yields the peaceful fruit of righteousness" (Hebrews 12:10-11).

He is not disciplining us because He does not like us. He says, "You are my sons; of course I love you. That is why I am whipping you into shape." It is a father who is really possessive of his child that the child will grow to maturity. He disciplines us in these spiritual matters and disciplines us in the matter of character until it is proven character with righteousness and holiness and peace without which no man will see the Lord. This is part of that discipline process, and along with the discipline process he also narrows the way of the racetrack.

SERVE THE PURPOSE OF GOD

As a matter of fact, as He brings us to maturity He narrows our ministry down to one—Him. I do not know if you have ever thought about that. I used to minister to a lot of people, but I have this funny feeling I am getting narrowed down because He is our Apostle, and we are to serve Him. He is the Head of the whole work thing, so we are to minister to Him, and then He will break our vessel and pour us out where He wants us to go. It is something when you are in Christian ministry and you are working for people in that association. These people are contributing but you do not know who you are serving. So here is the deal: serve only Him, the Apostle. Serve the Apostle, listen for His voice, get your directions from Him because if you are going to not just work works and serve the house of God, but you are going to serve the purpose of God then you have got to be sent out by the one Apostle who does God's work. All of the rest of the stuff is a lot of busyness some time that bears temporary fruit. But when we are narrowed down to serving our one Lord, the One with whom we have to do, then He sends us on a life poured out more than we ever knew when we are ministering to people and the house because the Lord loves people. But in your maturation into sonship there has to be an exclusive relationship between you and the Lord.

OUTSIDE THE CAMP

This leads us to the third part of this which is that He takes you outside the camp. Now He does not take you outside the camp when you read it. Actually what it says is that you go out to Him and He is outside the camp. So it is not a question of saying to somebody, "You need to leave that church; it is the camp." You do not have to bother with any of that. You just say, "Follow the Lamb wherever He goes," and if you do that you will find yourself outside the camp. It is not even worth trying to define what the camp is today. And it is not quite as easy as saying anything denominational is the camp; anything nondenominational is outside the camp. It is nothing like that. Some denominational people are more outside the camp than some people who are outside the denominations and are in the camp. These are shallow kind of things, but when you follow the Lord you find that you become someone who must bear some reproach because you are too simple. You see something and they say, "That will never work." You say, "That is what I saw; that is what I am going to do." And so you bear some reproach. Forever you will have to be explaining why you go to a place that does not have a pastor and all of those kinds of things. If you follow the Lord, you may have to suffer all kinds of things, but you share in the fellowship of His suffering from doing so. And so we grow and become sons through these various kinds of things.

Through our lives we live before the Lord, and through our lives we face disappointments and failures and things we thought were going to work but didn't, the church that is going well and then falls prey to attack in various ways and seems to disassemble and things get shaken. There are all of those kind of things. When you have a long history of that kind of thing, one of two things happens. Either you end up getting depressed and saying, "The whole thing is devastation. Just listen to your radio at nine in the morning and three in the afternoon where brother so and so will tell you why you should not go to church. Don't even talk to me about that church. It will never work. It never has; it never will. Every group I have ever seen has gone to seed in ten years."

The other thing that can happen is you come up with an answer that does not satisfy anybody but you and the Lord, and that is "But we see Jesus." He is our only hope for our own life. Here we are talking about bringing many sons to glory. Well, we have about three hundred prospects right here, and there is a long way to go, isn't it? We have tasted the wilderness dust plenty of times. Are we ever going to make it? "But we see Jesus." This has to be our hope. There is a Man in the glory, and He made it in and offered us this great salvation that when we run He runs with us, that when we are going into glory, He carries us into glory. We begin to live by His life, trusting Him for our whole provision. *We see Jesus.*

I know the Lord wants to bring us to sonship, and the Holy Spirit is working upon us even now towards that end. May we cooperate with Him in these last days for Jesus' sake. Amen.

.

Other Books Printed By
Christian Testimony Ministry

SPEAKER	TITLE
DANA CONGDON	MARRIAGE, SINGLENESS, AND THE WILL OF GOD
	RECOVERY & RESTORATION
	THE HOLY SPIRIT
	HEBREWS
A.J. FLACK	TENT OF HIS SPLENDOUR
STEPHEN KAUNG	ACTS
	BE YE THEREFORE PERFECT
	CALLED OUT UNTO CHRIST
	CALLED TO THE FELLOWSHIP OF GOD'S SON
	DIVINE LIFE AND ORDER
	FOR ME TO LIVE IS CHRIST
	GLORIOUS LIBERTY OF THE CHILDREN OF GOD
	GOD'S PURPOSE FOR THE FAMILY
	I WILL BUILD MY CHURCH
	MEDITATIONS ON THE KINGDOM
	RECOVERY
	SPIRITUAL EXERCISE
	SPIRITUAL LIFE (II CORINTHIANS SERIES)
	TEACH US TO PRAY
	THE CROSS
	THE FULNESS OF CHRIST—IN THE BOOK OF REVELATION
	THE HEADSHIP OF CHRIST
	THE KINGDOM AND THE CHURCH
	THE KINGDOM OF GOD
	THE LAST CALL TO THE CHURCHES, THE CALL TO OVERCOME
	THE LIFE OF OUR LORD JESUS
	THE LIFE OF THE CHURCH, THE BODY OF CHRIST
	THE LORD'S TABLE
	TWO GUIDEPOSTS FOR INHERITING THE KINGDOM
	VISION OF CHRIST (REVELATION)
	WHO ARE WE?

WHY DO WE SO GATHER?
WORSHIP

LANCE LAMBERT   CALLED UNTO HIS ETERNAL GLORY
                      GOD'S ETERNAL PURPOSE
                      IN THE DAY OF THY POWER
                      JACOB I HAVE LOVED
                      LIVING FAITH
                      LESSONS FROM THE LIFE OF MOSES
                      LOVE DIVINE
                      MY HOUSE SHALL BE A HOUSE OF PRAYER
                      PREPARATION FOR THE COMING OF THE LORD
                      REIGNING WITH CHRIST
                      SPIRITUAL CHARACTER
                      THE GOSPEL OF THE KINGDOM
                      THE IMPORTANCE OF COVERING
                      THE LAST DAYS AND GOD'S PRIORITIES
                      THE PRIZE
                      THE SUPREMACY OF JESUS CHRIST
                      THINE IS THE POWER!
                      THOU ART MINE

T. AUSTIN-SPARKS   THE LORD'S TESTIMONY AND THE WORLD NEED

HARVEY CEDARS CONFERENCE

STEPHEN KAUNG   HEAVENLY VISION
                      SPIRITUAL RESPONSIBILITY

CONGDON, HILE, KAUNG   SPIRITUAL MINISTRY
                      SPIRITUAL AUTHORITY
                      SPIRITUAL HOUSE
                      SPIRITUAL SUBMISSION

STEPHEN KAUNG   SPIRITUAL KNOWLEDGE
                      SPIRITUAL POWER
                      SPIRITUAL REALITY
                      SPIRITUAL VALUE
                      SPIRITUAL BLESSING
                      SPIRITUAL DISCERNMENT

www.ingramcontent.com/pod-product-compliance
Lightning Source LLC
Chambersburg PA
CBHW061726020426
42331CB00006B/1117